# THE NEW AWAKENING

### Thoughts to Inspire, Empower, Enlighten, and Entertain

**By**
**Eric Allen**

author ~THE NEW WAY
The Ultimate Guide
for Personal Power

*Cover Photograph by Eric Allen*

# Contents

# *Introduction*

My intention has always been, and will always be, to help others to love and empower themselves. I am devoted to my fellow human beings, to their happiness and enlightenment. I am deeply honored by the thousands of friends around the world who have been enjoying my thoughts and teachings and have been inspired in a powerful, positive way.

These same thoughts, however, will no doubt ruffle the feathers of some. For those, I would suggest that this is the perfect opportunity to pause and consider why you react that way. It is the perfect time to step outside of yourself and see who you truly are.

How can you tell if your thoughts are true or false? How can you tell if your belief system is true or false?

If you can become angered by a difference in opinion about your religion, belief system, or concept of a God, you have not truly connected to your higher self or spirit. Our spiritual energy knows no fear or anger. Anger is a human invention, a false belief. One cannot be angry and at the same time be at peace or be one with Divine Source. Therefore, if anger in any degree is part of your belief system or thought process, it cannot be the truth.

When you are truly connected to Source, no matter how much others disagree with you, you can simply smile and move on. You can accept all opinions as just another path that someone wishes to walk. You never take it as an attack on your group or personal belief system.

Remember:

*Enlightened beings do not condemn others for having different beliefs. Enlightened beings do not threaten others with eternal suffering. They understand that those who do are the ones who live in fear and darkness.*

All that I share is what I know, feel, and believe. If it rings true for you, embrace it. If it does not, discard it.

This book contains hundreds of my personal thoughts and sayings about *Life, Love, Sex, Religion, God (gods), Spirituality,* and so on. You will get them or you won't. You will agree with them or you won't. Either way, I hope that you spend some time thinking about them.

My goal has never been to convince anyone of anything. All I do is offer a different way of looking at ourselves and the world around us.

I, as many before me, have a great desire and passion to help those who are beginning to awaken; those who are realizing that there is another way; those who are ready to walk the path of *self-responsibility* and *self-empowerment*. As you have chosen to read this book, I know you must feel the same way.

We are all bright-eyed students and wonderful teachers. Together we will make great positive changes in the world. So please sit back, relax, open your mind, and enjoy.

~ Namaste ~

# *Acknowledgement*

Deepest gratitude to my wife, best friend and confidant, for showing me the true meaning of unconditional love for over 20 years. And to my daughter, an amazing 'old soul' who continues to teach me more about myself than I could ever have imagined. Thank you both for walking this 'road less travelled' with me. I love you with all my heart and every part of my being.

*You are a Magnificent Being. You are the physical manifestation of Spiritual Energy. You are ONE and the same with the powers that created the Universe. Your knowledge and experience is infinite.*

*You are the Source. You are the Creator of the life you are living. You are the Power you've been searching for.*

*How do I know this?*

*How do you not?*

\* \* \*

# *Part 1*

\* \* \*

# *Waking Up*

*The human race seriously needs to WAKE UP. How wonderful if it could be done with a Gentle Kiss. However, there will always be those who need a Gentle Push out of bed.*

\* \* \*

H ave you ever tried to awaken a child and get them ready for school? They moan and groan and pull the covers over their heads. They just want to slip back into the comfort of the darkness, the security of the womb.

They have, unfortunately, learned and developed many fears and anxieties. They have little or no desire to face the challenges of the world. You may try reasoning with the child, but they'll just pull the covers around them more tightly. Oh sure, you can just rip the covers off. But, now you have a child who is not only filled with fear and anxiety, but anger—not the healthiest way to start the day!

Most adults haven't changed much from childhood in this respect. In fact, their fears and anxieties have been ingrained much more deeply through years of practice. They need to jar themselves out of bed with an alarm, down some stimulant to pry their eyes open and then, usually with the same resentment as the child, head off into the day.

In essence, they continue to pull the covers over their heads. They create the illusion of being awake by programming themselves to function on a very low level. Most people are just getting by, totally unaware, just existing, living false beliefs, and being controlled and manipulated by fear. They're walking in their sleep.

For centuries, most of us on this planet have remained asleep; we walk around in a state of mass hypnosis. Our false beliefs have become our reality. In my first book, I refer to these beliefs as *Earth Plane Propaganda*, as I do for any manufactured belief system that prevents us from recognizing the perfection of who we truly are.

But, until one recognizes that they are asleep, there's very little chance of waking up. This is the greatest denial on our planet. And often, even those of us who start to open our eyes find the challenge ahead far too overwhelming to continue.

Why? Because to wake up would mean that everything we've been taught—who we are, the world around us, religion, God, and so on—will change. To many, this would be emotionally shattering.

Followers of religious and superstitious thoughts and beliefs are held in a powerful grip. They are always kept in fear of being punished for doing the 'wrong' thing. Would you break this grip and free yourself if you strongly believed that doing so would send you to an eternal place of pain and suffering when you die?

This is why most people have no desire to change the path they're on, even though their most powerful spiritual or gut instinct is telling them to do so. These denied feelings, of course, are one's true nature trying to push its way out. This true nature— the connection to Source or Spirit—is trying to guide them in a different direction, but their fear usually wins out. They will rationalize their true feelings as false or evil and pull the covers back over their heads.

Over thousands of years, mankind has created many powerful illusions of the world. These illusions have, of course, become reality. Throughout history, we have observed the behavior of those who are asleep; those firmly attached to organized belief systems. For thousands of years, they have fought and killed others who have tried to show them another way.

Today millions of people continue to be tortured and killed around the world in the name of religion. The people doing the killing are completely disconnected from the true powers of the Universe. Their lives are completely void of joy and so they create a 'God' that justifies their horrific actions. These people are in the deepest sleep. Their lives are based on fear.

The true essence of the Universe, however, is based on trust and love.

All wars, whether religious or political, are the actions of those in a deep sleep. How did we get this way?

Understandably, many of us here have become so completely attached to our bodies that we have forgotten that we are actually the physical manifestations of spirit. We have become disconnected. The more disconnected we become, the easier it is to be programmed to see ourselves as weak, fragile, and dependant, not the Amazing, Brilliant, Powerful Energies of Light and Love that we truly are.

We have allowed our egos to take over. Fear, anxiety, insecurity, doubt, lack, frustration, and so on, have become our way of life. Therefore, most of us are not fully enjoying our experience here on Earth. We would like things to be different, but we've been brainwashed to think that we have no choice.

But, we do have a choice. If you'd like to enjoy this experience more fully or on a higher level, if you'd like to manifest more love, joy, and happiness, it can become your reality. Right now, in this moment.

If, however, you feel that your journey here is to suffer and be miserable, then so be it. That too is your reality, and the Universe will support your choice. I am only here to tell you that you absolutely have options.

Please understand that waking up is not about fighting or rebelling against religions or our societies, or even about fighting yourself. Rebelling and fighting are for those that are still asleep. It is, however, about breaking the rules.

Now, I am all for following the 'laws' that we've created in our society. But, you must break through the constraints of the mental and emotional 'rules' that have been preventing you from awakening and creating your dreams.

There are no rules for Spirituality and Enlightenment. There are no limits within your mind and spirit. However, the rules of society, the rules of religion, and the rules of politics are all designed to keep you asleep.

Society's rules dictate how you should look and what you should buy or own to be accepted. Elective surgery to 'improve' breasts, noses, and so forth is skyrocketing. Yes, our society keeps you so deeply asleep you can't possibly recognize your own perfection. You are constantly told that you must change yourself, that you're never good enough. Keeping you asleep is big business.

Religion is another big business that does not want you to wake up. You must follow specific dogma and doctrines or be punished. Your mind is not your own and neither is your body. They will tell you that it belongs to a supreme being. And this being does not want you to do certain things with the body that you yourself actually created. Guilt and fear keep the money flowing.

Political correctness has continued to tighten the rope on your freedom. You are told what you can and can't say, even how you can say it. Everyone is becoming more and more sensitive, more and more weak and frightened. One day you can use a certain word and the next day you're told it's wrong. We've all become terrified of words, of mere sounds: the 'F' word, 'N' word, 'P' word, 'B' word, and 'C' word. We're going to run out of letters in the alphabet!

Everyone uses these words, yet we've been programmed to think they're offensive. We've given words incredible power over us, haven't we? As long as we give away our power we remain asleep. On almost every level of living we are giving up our power. To awaken we must be free.

YOU must be free. But, first you need to be willing to accept that what you've been taught is not the only way or the right way. You must also understand that the Universe does NOT punish anyone for seeking enlightenment.

You then need to learn to be perfectly honest with yourself. This requires you taking a long look at everything that has NOT been working in your life, whether it is religion, marriage, health, relationship, family, friend, or work related. You will need to throw the covers off and expose your deepest fears and weaknesses.

Yet, this is what most of you dread. Many of you feel that life is tough enough without having to add more heavy emotions to it. Sure, no one wants to open the proverbial can of worms. But, in order to make life easier you must sometimes go through a period of greater challenges.*

[*Note my intentional use of the word challenges, *as opposed to* pain and suffering. *Challenges are valuable lessons. Pain and suffering imply blame. More about this in the chapter on* Responsibility.]

Although these challenges may seem overwhelming at times, they will always bring about a heightened awareness. It is this heightened awareness or higher level of consciousness that kick starts the waking up process. This is the road to self-empowerment. This is the road to true freedom.

But, it's certainly understandable that many will see this as a tough and frightening road. After all, it is a 'breaking down' process. You will be going through a major transitional period, a time when you will feel very vulnerable. Perhaps you will be wondering if you're doing the right thing. Many will want to duck back under the covers.

The greatest setbacks occur when friends and family can't or won't accept the fact that you're changing. All of us who have started to awaken have had to deal with this. Friends will move away, family members will laugh at you or even express anger. Most people don't have the courage to walk this 'road less traveled'. This I understand very well.

I personally have walked the same path for most of my life. But, I have never been interested in having many friends as much as having a few who are like-minded, fun, free thinking, powerful, politically in-correct, and non-religious spiritual beings.

Just remember this: *As you truly awaken, you may find yourself alone at times, but you will never feel lonely.*

The powerful energy that flows through you is all you will need for true happiness and joy. You will understand and experience life on a much higher level. You will start to experience levels of happiness and joy you could not have imagined before. And then you will start to attract others who have also started to walk this path.

Your views on religion and God/Source will cer-tainly change drastically as you come to understand and appreciate that you truly are the creator of your life. You will come to know the true meaning of Spirituality.

*Open your mind*
*to the wisdom of the heavens*
*and set yourself free*

\* \* \*

# *God*

# *Religion*

# *Spirituality*

\* \* \*

One day, many years ago, my wife and I took our ten year old daughter and her friend to an amusement park. I looked up at one of the mega roller coasters and remarked, "Oh my, God," to which the little girl replied, "Mr. Allen, you just used God's name in vain."

My wife and I looked at each other in both amazement and amusement. I was torn between bursting out in laughter or giving this little tyke the biggest lecture of her life. Of course, my spirit resisted both.

It did, however, make me think about all the religious thoughts and concepts designed to control children with fear and take their power away. How sad to raise our children with such unfounded fears.

How sad to control and manipulate a child's mind into believing there is someone 'up there' who is concerned about the most insignificant and trivial details of how his name is used.

At the earliest age, many children are taught that there is a supreme being, usually a man, who constantly needs to be adored and worshipped. So, their first introduction to God is that he is an all-powerful spirit with a huge ego. He also wants them to make sure they capitalize the 'G' in his name, and most importantly, put a hyphen (G-d) instead of an 'o' because, well, I guess this 'All Powerful Being' is very easily bothered by people using his complete name. In other words, he has anger and control issues. And that's just the beginning.

Now, if they don't follow all these rules he will punish them severely and will not let them into a very special place when they die. They are told that this being will constantly test them in the most horrible ways imaginable, so he can see if they have faith in him ... A being who will allow wars, rape, murder, starvation, poverty, and more because, well, they are perhaps not worshipping him enough or correctly. Or maybe he just needed a little time off because, once again, he's angry at us.

Is it any wonder that the world is in the state it's in? Is it any wonder that people's lives are not working on most levels? Is it any wonder that we live in a fearful, angry world where we don't love and respect each other? Not really.

Religions depend upon their followers. The best way to keep followers from drifting away is to keep them afraid, very afraid. So man created 'God' to control the masses—a cruel god who sits back and watches us suffer, just because he feels like it. He could easily put a stop to all this suffering, but no, he feels that we need it, that it's necessary for our growth.

Of course, it's silly. Of course, it's absurd. And the more we awaken the sillier it seems.

*How did the Beautiful, Powerful, Positive, Loving energy of the Universe become a cruel, arrogant, egotistical, manipulative, and controlling being?*

*Because man created God in his image, not the other way around.* God has become a reflection of man's weaknesses and fears. And in doing so, mankind has continued to create even greater weaknesses and complications over the centuries.

Why did this happen? The answer again is that we've become disconnected from our Loving Source or

Spiritual Energy. We have forgotten who and what we truly are. We have forgotten that we are ONE and the SAME with this Grand Intelligent Loving Energy that created the Universe.

All enlightened teachers will help us to understand that we all hold the same key; that we all have access to the same incredible abundance of knowledge that every past master had before us.

The more you start to remember this, the less and less you will need to seek outside of yourself for answers. This is the beauty of True Spirituality. We truly are one with the Universe. Know it. Feel it. Believe it.

We are all from the same Source. We are all the same Energy, experiencing life in various physical forms. The more we have become attached to our physical forms, however, the further we have moved away from understanding or experiencing the Energy or Source from which we came.

We started looking outside of ourselves, or up to the sky, rather than within. As we lost touch with our powers we started to believe in powers that are separate from ourselves. So, man created all forms of gods, and often just one God.

Man, of course, attached his own personality to God. Each culture created a god that looks, feels, and has experiences based on that culture. How could man do otherwise? This is man's ego expressing itself.

As enlightened beings we ask ourselves a couple of questions. Why would such a creative, loving and beautiful spiritual energy judge and punish anyone for simply not agreeing? If your child grew up to have different beliefs than you, would you try to find ways to sabotage that child's life? Would you abuse that child and create ways for that child to suffer endlessly until he/she finally broke down, gave in, and followed your path? What kind of person would that make you?

To give any credence to the idea that a supreme being would allow so many atrocities to occur in this world, allow so much dysfunctional behavior, and then to make excuses for that being is certainly a product of our being asleep, of living in fear.

This is also a direct insult to the grand, powerful, beautiful spiritual energy that we are all a part of—a grand insult to the Universe and, maybe more importantly, a grand insult to *yourself*.

Only man's huge, insecure ego could create a being so arrogant, so horrifying, and so frightening.

This is not Universal Energy. This is not Spiritual Energy. This is not the Source. This is not the Truth. For when you truly connect to Source, when you finally awaken, you will come to understand that the Universe is always for you, never against you. You will come to realize that you are responsible for your life. You are the creator and the energy that flows through you is the same Universal Intelligence shared by all. If the word *God* makes you happier, then by all means enjoy it. The name or label does not matter.

Either way, there is no one 'up there' looking down on you in judgment.

The ***Spiritual Energy or 'God'*** is within you. Or, it might be more appropriate to say, that there is ***GODLINESS within you***.

Think of the Universe as one massive cosmic brain that has been evolving for billions and billions of years, its thoughts creating or manifesting any energy in any form that any of us could possibly imagine. No limitations.

Imagine every one of us tapped into this Cosmic Brain. Not separate from it, but one with it.

Expand your thinking. Don't think *size* or *scale* or *time* or *place*. We are the Universe. YOU are the Universe. The Universe is us.

And this is why the Universe will grant whatever you like, depending on the clarity and power of your intention. But, you must free your mind. Most of us don't know how to do that. They don't teach that in our schools or places of worship. No one can *Free* their mind as long as they remain followers of a *Closed* belief system.

The only way to free your mind is to completely give up the limiting thoughts and beliefs you are now attached to, the ones that have been holding you back. And that is the great challenge for most on this planet. Fear has kept most of us prisoners inside our own minds.

So, perhaps it's time to start looking at yourself differently. You are not just a pawn put down here to be played with. You are an extension of this great powerful force. You *are* this great powerful force. You are here to have any experience you desire, and after you leave, your magnificent energy will flow on to other wonderful, beautiful places, planes, and dimensions.

You are infinite. You are timeless. You are the *Power*. You are the *Creator*. If you want to see God ... look in the mirror.

# Responsibility
# Part I

\* \* \*

Although I wrote about responsibility in my first book, it is so incredibly important that I decided to expound further upon it here.

The statement,

*'We are completely responsible*

*for the lives we are living,'*

continues to be a bold statement that creates so much resistance.

And understandably so, since most people believe that they have no control over the circumstances in their lives. Most have been taught that their lives are in the hands of everyone and everything around them; they are just billiard balls being banged into one another.

It's so easy to blame someone else or even the Universe when things are not going the way you'd like them to go, isn't it?

*My marriage is failing because of him/her.*

*I'm angry and hurt because of ...*

*I can't get anything done because of ...*

*My life would be happier if it wasn't for ...*

The list goes on and on.

If you'd like to change your life from the position of being a victim to becoming completely self-empowered, you must change this way of thinking.

***Your thoughts are energies that directly affect who you are and what you create and attract in your life.***

Here's a suggestion: Eliminate *BLAME* from your vocabulary.

*Can anyone really make you angry?*

*Can anyone really make you insecure?*

*Can anyone really make you do something that you don't want to do?*

*Can anyone really make you feel sad?*

**Absolutely NOT!**

Everything in life is a choice. Every 'negative' reaction you have is a choice based on a false truth that you've been taught and incorporated into your own belief system.

You must understand that everything happening in your life is in perfect alignment with what you are thinking, feeling, and believing at your deepest subconscious level—thought patterns that may go all the back to your childhood and beyond.

You, therefore, will continue to create certain circumstances until you become aware of these thought patterns—circumstances that your spirit *needs* in order to evolve to the next level.

Everything that you create is in essence a 'wake up call.' There is no such thing as a bad lesson. It's all for your highest good.

Let's take, for example, the very common expression, "He/she broke my heart." How many times have you used this expression or heard it from others?

And it goes on. "He lied to me." "She cheated on me." "I gave everything to him and he let me down." It was always the other person's fault, right? NO.

"Wait a minute," you say. "So, you're telling me I attracted the person who 'broke my heart'?"

Yes, of course. In fact, your heart is not broken at all. What you're feeling are growing pains, massive changes, important changes, realizations that you are not who you thought you were. It is actually a fantastic opportunity for enlightenment and growth. But, most of us have learned to fear change. We have learned to view it as heartbreak or misery.

Actually, you should be grateful to the person who lied to you or cheated on you. It was a gift. It was exactly what you needed to wake yourself up. You attracted this situation for that very reason.

Understanding this, you are now able to release that person with *love* and move on to the next level. Remember, if you continue to hold on to them in an angry way, you remain stuck as a victim and cannot grow or move forward.

You are not a victim. You're a beautiful, powerful, evolving spirit. Claim your power and move on.

And what about those whom you release? It doesn't matter. You're wasting precious energy thinking about them. Their lessons are entirely their own now. Believe me; they will have their own set of consequences to deal with. Those who choose to lie or deceive have a most challenging road ahead. They will, undoubtedly, go from one dysfunctional relationship to another until they've learned *their* lessons.

Remember:

***Enlightenment is as much about creating wonderful relationships as it is about knowing when to release the ones that are not working.***

This is *freedom*. This is taking *responsibility*.

What about blaming your parents or those who raised you? Are they to blame for who you are?

Absolutely not. You chose them. Yes, once again you all attracted each other. All of the sadness and anger that you may be holding onto serves no purpose. No one is to blame. If your parents were highly dysfunctional they could only have raised you on the level of their experiences. These experiences were passed down to them from their dysfunctional parents. Unfortunately, they didn't have the tools to change their behavior.

If the parents are not capable of learning and evolving, it then becomes the responsibility of the adult child to evolve so that the dysfunction is not passed on again.

The anger toward the parents should be released. Our empowerment comes from recognizing that they were not evil or monsters, just unenlightened, weak, frightened, and insecure.

How do we deal with other people's anger toward us? This is also our responsibility. Never take someone else's anger personally. As we become more enlightened we can see clearly that the root of anger is always *fear*. How would you deal with a frightened child? With compassion and understanding. I'm not saying it's easy. This is our challenge, to not allow ourselves to be caught up in someone else's drama.

It takes much courage and strength. But, this is also our responsibility as enlightened beings. This is why I always stress *self-empowerment*. We can't help others until we've learned to help ourselves. And, yes, I agree that there are times we must walk away. Each person and each situation is unique. Just know that everything is a lesson. Everything is a Grand Opportunity to learn something about ourselves.

It's time for each of us to be responsible for our own lives.

# Responsibility
# Part II
# Sickness, Illness, and Disease

\* \* \*

Now, if you're starting to understand that *we are the Masters of our thoughts and the Creators of the lives we are living,* it's time to move on to another heated and controversial subject.

We are responsible for everything in our lives including sickness, illness, and disease.

You can imagine how much anger and confusion this causes. When I encourage others to 'take responsibility' in these areas, I am often challenged with, "How can you tell a child or an adult with cancer or some other 'dreaded' disease that they are *to blame* for whatever they have? Don't you know that it will only make them feel worse and fill them with guilt?"

And here lies the dilemma. The words *blame* and *guilt* are always thrown about when talking about responsibility. But, blame and guilt are not in my vocabulary. Blame and guilt will always weaken someone. It will always take their power away. What I am talking about is raising one's consciousness to a higher level by taking responsibility.

To take responsibility is completely and totally empowering. It is to understand that everything in life is just a lesson.

*When you can view illness or disease as a lesson, you have already turned it into something positive ... and something positive will help you, not hurt you.*

Blame, however, is the exact opposite. Blame implies you did something wrong; something you should feel guilty about; something you are being punished for. There is no need for guilt in getting sick. Sickness can be a blessing if we use it to guide us into a more positive and powerful way of thinking. That, of course, is why we created it in the first place.

All illnesses and diseases are simply the manifestations of negative thoughts that we haven't been aware of. The illness brings it to our attention. Drugs won't help us to see these thoughts. However, honesty, openness, and looking within will enlighten us and heal us.

Why do diseases come back? The drugs or surgeries are quick fixes. But, they haven't dealt with the real reasons for getting sick in the first place.

Now, the reality is, most people are not going to give up their medications and surgeries. Nor can we expect them to. Their fear is every bit as real as those who thought they would fall off the edge of the world centuries ago. It will take many, many years of convincing for this type of thought process to sink in and for people to actually start incorporating it into their mental and emotional belief system.

It's the same as Peace on Earth. Will it happen tomorrow? No, but that doesn't mean we shouldn't start teaching our children to be peaceful and loving. Or should we throw our arms up in the air and continue to teach hopelessness and fear? No. It's time to wake up.

It's time to wake up and start teaching responsibility on every level, including our health. Start teaching your children, not only how to heal sickness, but how to prevent it from happening in the first place. What a wonderful, powerful gift you would be giving.

But, of course this brings on the fearful argument that people have been programmed to use: "What about children with cancer? And, if parents don't allow the surgery and give the medication that the doctors prescribe, their child will die." They always end this argument with, "Then, how would you feel if that was you?"

There is tremendous guilt and fear in this argument. You can't easily change the thinking of people who feel this way. It's too powerful. And this is why we are not changing. Our fears have been very deeply embedded in our minds.

Of course, there is nothing anyone can do or say for people who think this way. All you can do is support their choice for surgeries and medication ... and that's okay. After all, it's just a choice. If you believe strongly enough that surgery and medication will heal you, it probably will.

If, however, you believe that you can heal yourself, this will be *your Truth*.

This is how powerful you are. This is the power that you have when you tap into your Higher Level of

Consciousness. This is the power you understand when you Awaken.

## *What is disease really?*

Every thought we think, millions and millions of thoughts a day (many we're not even aware of), are buried deeply within our minds. All of these thoughts are energies that create a certain frequency or vibration.

These vibrations are absorbed into every cell in our body. So, trillions and trillions of cells are absorbing our conscious and subconscious thoughts all day long, every day, even in our sleep.

Many of these thoughts are of fear, anxiety, anger, pain and insecurity—thoughts that we've probably been carrying with us from our childhood.

The cells in our body don't judge these thoughts. They don't change the thoughts; they simply absorb them. And the length of time these vibrations continue, and the level at which they are resonating, will determine how the cells will be affected.

Over time, the cells will start to change or mutate. It is in this way that our bodies start to show symptoms of illness or disease. Most of us don't understand these changes. We've been taught that they 'just' happen all by themselves. But they don't.

All the medical profession does is look at the changes in the body. They don't understand where these changes originated. That's not their concern. So, they will develop drugs to slow down or stop the changes. But, in doing so, these drugs will damage other cells in other ways.

A medical fact, by the way, is that every single drug developed by man, and I stress *every* single drug, has contraindications, meaning they all have some negative side-effects, many of them deadly.

Now, because we have so many different thoughts (because there are so many unique individuals), throughout history we have continued to create new diseases. And with each new illness, the pharmaceutical industry creates more drugs and/or new surgeries.

But, what we need in reality is to go within, to clear our minds, pinpoint our negative thoughts, and then understand where they have come from. And once we get in touch with these thoughts, we change the vibration which has mutated or changed these cells with a new healthier vibration through creating new positive thought patterns. As the cells start resonating with the energy vibration of these new thoughts, they will change again. They will change back to what they were originally—healthy, happy, joy-filled cells. And this is how we reverse disease or heal ourselves.

We now know that children are affected by the thoughts and actions of their parents while still in the womb. Whatever the mother is thinking, feeling, or physically putting into her body is all being absorbed into the cells of the child.

Once the child is born it, of course, has no awareness of the energy it has absorbed. But, it will start to develop physical and emotional patterns based on the energy it had received.

A child's illness may very well be the most important lesson for all involved—the parents and child. Everyone has the opportunity to learn and become empowered.

Again, there is no one to blame for anything. We are all doing exactly what we are capable of doing at each level of our evolution. And I believe, without a doubt, that the spirit of the child chose the parents for a particular lesson.

So, is it too much to ask ourselves to *take responsibility* for every aspect of our lives?

The reality is that all sickness, illness, and diseases *can* be cured by taking responsibility for our physical, mental, and emotional states.

But, here's the challenge. How long does it take to change the consciousness of the masses? How long did it take to convince people that the Earth was round? How long did it take to convince the masses that we could fly? We are still so primitive on so many levels. Dealing with illness is one of those levels.

Remember that we're dealing with a society based on money, not spirituality. And Big Pharmaceutical Corporations are not ready to give up $900 BILLION of drug business. It is not in their best interest to teach us how to heal ourselves. We're on our own.

Little by little, however, top medical professionals are finding the courage to come forward and blast the old ways of thinking. They are proving, with the most modern technology, that disease is just another imbalance of energy. Cancer is just another energy that has no more power over us than a cold. And this energy can be corrected with thoughts and diet, not drugs and surgery.

I would refer you to people like Bruce Lipton PhD, James Oschman PhD, Deepak Chopra PhD as just a few who are leading the way. You may also view CDs like the *The Living Matrix* or *Cancer is Curable Now.* The world is not flat.

# Love

\* \* \*

There is no power greater than *love*. Yet, it is the most misunderstood and abused word in our language.

We first learn about love through fairytales. The man, usually a knight or prince, needs to save a woman, either poor or a princess, who is always helpless.

Later, we learn from romance novels that love is all about sex and lust and leaving all sensibilities behind.

Soaps show us that love is always highly dysfunctional and that relationships are nothing but lies and deceit.

Magazines have degraded love to a form of hunting, teaching us special techniques to capture, control, and keep a mate from escaping.

Self-help books try to convince us that all women want one thing and all men want another thing. You know, men are from one planet and women from another.

And let's not forget all those wonderful 'love' songs, such as: 'love stinks,' 'love hurts,' 'only love can break your heart,' 'I can't live without you, so lonely I wanna die,' 'you're nobody till somebody loves you,' and most recently, a song that would have you 'jump in front of a train' and 'take a bullet in the brain' for love.

Wow, is it any wonder that both sexes are confused and frustrated and that relationships are failing at a higher rate than ever before?

We've learned to confuse love with infatuation, addiction, compulsiveness, neediness, and even abuse. So, what is love and how do we know it when we see it?

First, we need to stop looking at love as a thing—something we can get or give or take or control or manipulate or find somewhere. We really need to *stop searching* for it.

> *You can search the world for Love and you will NEVER find it. If, however, you learn to LOVE YOURSELF, then Love will always find you.*

Love is not a process of searching through dating sites, magazines, clubs, or in exotic lands. It is the process of working on oneself to find a higher level of *self-confidence* and *self-empowerment*—a level where you are perfectly comfortable to be alone. It is at this level where you connect to your Source, which is, in fact, *love.*

We unfortunately are not taught this as children. We're fed the unrealistic idea, the fantasy, that we are not complete without a partner.

Nothing could be further from the truth. No one can ever complete you. No one ever will. And no one ever should. As long as you feel that someone else will complete you, you will never be whole and complete. You will always be dependent. You will always be weak, and you will always be a victim.

You'll continue to give up your power to this person in fear that they will leave. How can you not? You have made THEM your source of love.

Once you have learned to love yourself, you will undoubtedly be a magnet for others who also love themselves. This is what love is truly about. Love is about sharing our completeness and wholeness with each other, not about giving or taking to fill empty spaces within ourselves.

*We are stars shining beautifully and brightly. Each one of us is beaming with our own brilliance and, at the same time, admiring each other's magnificence.*

When one or the other is lacking self-love there will always be an unbalanced relationship. This is how we confuse love with neediness or addiction. Where one is trying to fill their emptiness there can be no real joy. There will always be insecurity, manipulation, and disappointment.

Love cannot really be given to anyone. But, the *power of love* can certainly be felt and shared.

The power of love can heal others; not by giving others your love, but by making others aware of the love within themselves. We are all the same energy. When we heal others with love we simply help them to open those channels that they may have been blocking.

And this is how we change the world. The more we fill ourselves with the power of love the more others start to become aware of this power for themselves.

But, it's a double-edged sword. At first, those of us who are resonating with love are often looked at as odd. We are told that we can't be real, that we must be living in a fantasy world. This is how difficult it is for most beings to comprehend the power of love.

Nevertheless, we must understand and embrace those who have not yet found this power of love within. Of course, it doesn't seem real to them. How could it? It must be experienced to be understood. Those of us who feel it deeply within our core are passionate about sharing this feeling with others.

So, how will you know when love is real?

Everything will look different to you. You will see beauty where others see ugliness. You will see light where others see darkness. All apprehension will turn into excitement. You will be fearless as a lion and secure enough to cry at a sunset. You will have the power to enjoy sensitivity and openness, while others remain blocked and protective. You will have the power to manifest your fondest dreams. You will truly know happiness.

This is the *Ultimate Power of Love.*

# Gratitude

*＊＊

W hat exactly is *gratitude,* and who are you thanking if there's no one up there sitting on a cloud?

Gratitude is our magical connection to that most Grand Power in the Universe, *love.*

Remember that you are powerful energy and every thought you think is a powerful vibration that directly affects what you create in your life. The Universe does not judge. You plant the seed; the Universe will make sure it grows.

*Your mind is a Magical Garden. EVERYTHING you put in it will grow.*

*What are you planting today?*

*Fear or Excitement?*

*Doubt or Confidence?*

*Frustration or Patience?*

*Hate or Love?*

*Plant a garden for your*

*SPIRIT to Blossom.*

When you express gratitude you are thanking the Universe for complying with your thoughts. You are saying, in essence, that you understand that there is no right or wrong. You are accepting things the way they are. You are grateful that the Universe is always in perfect alignment with your level of thought or vibration. This creates a harmonious relationship with the Universe, rather than one of resistance. You create a more powerful love relationship.

*The more powerful your love relationship is between yourself and the Universe, the more in tune you will be to manifest your desires.*

So, what if you're in the midst of some seemingly overwhelming challenges? You might not feel there is anything to be grateful for. In fact, you may want to lash out at someone or the Universe with anger.

It is necessary to realize that it was your thoughts or vibrations that created these challenges in the first place. Yes, it's back to *responsibility*.

If you express anger, the Universe does not judge your emotional outbreak. It simply recognizes that this is a particular energy you are vibrating with. As far as the Universe is concerned, you must like this angry energy because you're making the conscious choice to express it. The Universe complies by giving you more anger and frustration.

This is the beauty and the magic of the Universe. It will always match your intention or desire. It will always give you what you are most strongly resonating with.

So, now you can understand how important it is to show gratitude, not just for the wonderful manifestations, but for the challenging situations as well. After all, once you have released the anger you will surely learn an empowering, enlightening lesson. It *is* all for your highest good.

By showing gratitude, the Universe now sends back positive energy which allows you to change your thoughts or energy even more quickly.

And the more gratitude you express to the Universe, the more happiness and joy will flow through you. And the less and less you will deal with challenges and obstacles in the future.

Practicing gratitude is the key to creating the life you desire. It is truly the Magic Lamp. So, how do you practice?

Start by being grateful for everything, no matter how small, and no matter what situation you may be in at that moment. But, what if your perception is that things are really going badly in your life? So badly you just can't see any light?

There's a story of a concentration camp survivor who expressed gratitude for the fleas that infested her bed. The fleas, it seemed, kept the brutal guards from coming in and abusing her. So, she was actually able to turn what most of us would consider the most horrific situation into gratitude. And this is how she survived. If a human being at that level could change her thought process, don't you think you can?

Do you have clothes to wear today? Be grateful for that. Are you able to eat today? Thank the Universe for the food. Do you have a bed to sleep in? Can you walk or talk or see? You woke up this morning. Be grateful, always, for everything.

I wake up in the morning and thank the Universe for being able to experience a new day. I thank the Universe for my family, my home, my car, and my dog. I thank the Universe for the trees, the birds, the sky, the sun ... for everything! These are all glorious gifts. I am grateful from morning till night. It just feels so good. All this can be done in your mind, by the way. But, it's also nice to find a time of day to say thank you out loud if you're capable.

If this all sounds corny or silly to you, then you do not understand that you, and everything around you, are *miracles* to be grateful for.

The more you practice gratitude, the more light will start to shine in your life. The more you will connect and really start to appreciate every aspect of your experience.

This will, of course, start to open all the spiritual channels for a positive flow of energy. More and more *happiness, health, joy, peace,* and *prosperity* will start to manifest in your life. It's a wonderful cycle. The more gratitude you express, the more *abundance* you'll receive.

There is no limit as to how much happiness you can experience.

Express gratitude to the max.

# *Abundance*

*Abundance is not something you acquire. It's something you must recognize within yourself.*

*Abundance flows through you like the endless waves of the ocean. Love, Health, Happiness, Success, and Financial Wealth are just reflections of the Abundance within your Heart.*

*Let the Ocean of Abundance flow freely through your mind, body, and spirit.*

\* \* \*

*Y*ou can manifest anything you want in your life, no matter who you are.

I've always found it fascinating that people actually get angry when I tell them they can have whatever they desire. It's as though I am committing a crime. These are some standard responses/arguments:

*The Arguments...*

*So, are you telling me that with positive thinking everyone in the world can be a millionaire right now?*

*So, are you telling me that everyone in the world can have everything they want?*

*Aren't we a world of limited resources?*

*Where is everything going to come from if everyone can manifest anything they want?*

*So, are you telling me all I have to do is think some positive thoughts and I can have a mansion in Beverly Hills?*

I used to feel attacked when people would respond (or should I say, *react*) with such questions. But, I've come to understand how difficult it is for many to understand these concepts. If most people on this planet are not able to manifest what they want, to them it can only mean one thing: that I'm delusional.

Well, first of all, manifesting or creating a specific outcome is not just about thinking positive thoughts for a moment, or just saying some positive words. It's about completely changing your views, your opinions, your feelings, and your belief system.

And YES, once you do this, your desires have no limits. The verbal and written affirmations, or positive thoughts, are absolutely essential, but the affirmations are just stepping stones.

In the beginning, your mind will most likely resist and not want to believe an affirmation like, "I am wealthy and successful," especially if you've been creating great financial challenges. But, by saying it thousands of times in your head, your subconscious thoughts will start to align themselves with this new vibration.

Resonating with these new vibrations is the starting point. Remember that your subconscious has been resonating with thoughts of lack for many years. It takes time to reprogram your mind. This is where you will have to be diligent. You must bombard your mind with positive thoughts all day, every day. How willing are you to do that?

And how willing are you to change your belief system? How willing are you to STOP challenging the powers of the mind and spirit?

Just questioning the fact that we can have anything we want is a belief system all on its own. This powerful belief system, or *mindset* of *doubt*, exists at the very core of all who are suffering with pain, illness, starvation, or lack of any kind.

Let's take a look around us. We live in a world of *limited thinking*. And limited thinking has been producing limited results. We have programmed ourselves to view the world in a certain way. It is time for a new understanding.

For thousands of years, we have been diligently practicing thoughts of weakness and fear. The culmination of this is a world completely unbalanced. We have only a small portion of our societies enjoying abundance, while most of the world is struggling and starving.

It's first important to understand that abundance is not a thing that we can hold. It is, in fact, a powerful belief system. But, so is the feeling of *lack, the opposite of abundance*. And both have equal power.

If a person or society has been developing a *lack mentality* for a long time, believing they don't have the power to access what they need, they are not going to learn how to manifest incredible wealth instantly. Think how deeply we live in our belief systems. The chains of anger, blame, doubt, and fear are very strong.

Certainly, some beings have been able to make fantastic leaps from one level to the other. It is entirely and absolutely possible. It all depends on the individual's power of intention. But, for most it will take much smaller steps to evolve to that point. Again, it is up to you. And practice makes perfect.

First, you must understand that abundance or wealth is **how you feel about yourself**, not what you own. One can feel incredibly wealthy without any money at all. The wealth and abundance of *self-love* is infinitely more important than money and much more powerful. As I stated before, this is true happiness.

Of course, as you start to feel this abundance and wealth inside, you open yourself up to manifest wealth in other ways, such as attracting money, love, or whatever else you desire. This is *wealth consciousness*.

But, to get to this place you must change your thoughts about money or opulence. Think of the messages you are sending out to the Universe.

Do you say things like this? ...

*Money doesn't grow on trees.*

*The rich get richer and the poor get poorer.*

*Money is the root of all evil.*

*Rich people are no good.*

*Money is not spiritual.*

How can you expect to manifest abundance with a 'lack' consciousness? Do you really believe that money is not spiritual? NONSENSE. Money IS spiritual. Don't let anyone tell you otherwise. Money is just another form of energy. It becomes whatever thoughts you attach to it. Remember, money is as 'good' or 'bad' as the person holding it. Negative labeling will only block its flow to you. Start to apply positive energy to money.

Do you not give to charities because you 'can't' afford to? Wealthy people give to charities. So, just giving a few dollars, as if you *are* wealthy, can free you of this 'lack' mentality. No one will get hurt if you just start pretending to be wealthy in your own mind. Your mind will actually start to enjoy that feeling. Eventually, you will find more money, jobs, and other situations manifesting in your life. This is NOT a ridiculous notion. It works.

***Change your thoughts and***

***you will change your life.***

Now, let's talk about everybody on earth having a twenty room mansion with a huge pool. This, of course, is part of our limited thinking. Those who only understand lack in the world will always think about extreme 'earth plane' desires.

The reasons we have people with large mansions and people with absolutely nothing is because of the tremendous imbalance of energy we've created on this planet. Whenever minds create one extreme, other minds will create the opposite. It's human nature. This is all about the fighting, the winning, the pushing, and the pulling.

Imagine if you will, everyone on this planet filled completely with the feeling and power of *love* and *abundance*. Imagine each and every person truly understanding their own uniqueness and perfection, loving themselves deeply and wholly. Imagine every person able to live on a plane of existence where everything is always taken care of; there's no stress and no worry; there's always enough food, clothing, safety, security, and so on. Imagine no want in any way.

You would be free of attachments. There would be no one trying to outdo anyone else. You couldn't. The ego would have no place here. There would be no more 'mine is bigger than yours' mentality.

And most importantly, everyone would always make sure everyone else was manifesting on the same level.

Of course, most people on the planet will say this is impossible. It's absurd, a pipedream. Their eyes roll back, they scoff or get angry. Positive thinking is not popular in our culture. The intellectual mind says, "If you can't prove it scientifically, it cannot be done." And it is this type of thinking that will always prevent miracles from happening. For miracles are simply the manifestations of powerful positive beliefs. Perhaps this is the reason why most are not experiencing miracles in their lives.

I personally will continue to believe in the Grand Possibility of it all.

I will continue to imagine a world of Abundance.

How about you?

# *Peace Without War*

\* \* \*

Fighting for peace is just about the most ludicrous concept that man has created on this planet. But, the people who remain in power believe strongly that we must fight and kill others for peace and/or financial gain (greed).

To rebel against these powers, however, puts us on the same level as those we wish to change. If we lower our vibration to that level of mentality, we only hinder our own growth or spiritual evolution. That is not the energy conducive to anyone's enlightenment. Fighting or trying to gain power over others on any level is primitive and a giant step backwards.

We already have unlimited power within our minds. When we tap into this power we understand that there is never a need to fight. In fact, it is quite the opposite.

The real power comes to us by giving in or letting go. This is the *freeing* of the mind. When the mind is free it can release all the false beliefs that have caused us to engage in any conflict. And this is where we need to be if we are going to make any positive changes in the world.

When our mind becomes clear, detached from ego, it is truly free to fill itself with the energy of Source. You now know this energy is *love*—the most grand and powerful force in nature.

### *The Enlightened mind comes to understand that*

### *Gentleness is the Greatest Power for change.*

So, no matter what situations we find ourselves in, no matter what anyone is doing around us, we can always find this level of calm and peace within ourselves.

As more and more of us learn how to reach this level of 'being,' there is no doubt that it will eventually start having an effect on the rest of the world, including those in power who have been the most resistant.

This in no way means for us to be passive or to be in denial about the chaos in the world. We need to make these thoughts and feelings known. We need to constantly remind those around us. We need to speak up, not in protest, but with powerful passion. We need to be prime examples of Peaceful Power.

The great philosopher, Confucius, once decided to go live among a group of savages. His friends and colleagues questioned his sanity. Why would he do such a thing? Confucius replied, "How could they remain savages for long with a man like me living amongst them?"

The Truth is we do not need to fight others, nor force others to change. As larger and larger groups of us change our thinking processes, the greater the effect we will have on the world.

As a master martial artist the big question I'm always asked is, "If someone attacked you, would you fight back?"

In over forty years as a martial artist I'm proud to say I have never attracted that kind of energy in my life. All the punching and kicking techniques, which could easily kill another human being, are used only to destroy the ego of the practitioner. This is what separates a true master of the martial arts from the others. Learning how fragile the human body is gives me great respect for the power I yield. As an enlightened being, I use these powers only to reach higher levels of consciousness. It is said that the greatest samurai is one who never has to draw his sword. I believe the Peaceful Warriors will create the greatest, long lasting, positive changes in the world.

So, is your mind reeling with anger and frustration? Are you asking what should we do with the people in the world who embrace violence? What do we do about terrorists and so on? Are we just supposed to let them kill us? These questions are, of course, fear based. There could not be terrorists unless we lived in a world of fear. The more we fear the more reasons we have to fight. The more we fight, the more reasons we give ourselves to fear. Yes, we've been playing this game on our planet for a very long time.

I'm not here to say that these challenges will disappear tomorrow. I'm only here to say that these challenges will continue on the same exact path until we, as a collective consciousness, are willing to SEE things differently. Our societies have been raised with fear and war for thousands of years. And we continue to pass this legacy of fear, hatred, and anger to our children. How willing are you to teach your children differently?

Let's look at nature. If you run from a bear, it senses your fear and will attack. If you have no fear it will pass you by. There are some who can walk through a pit of rattlesnakes without a single disturbance. But, one fearful thought will cause them to strike. These are just two very small examples of how nature can teach us valuable life lessons. We are nature. Violent animals, human or otherwise, are simply experiencing a lower level of consciousness. To create a peaceful world we must learn to raise our consciousness and transcended fear, anger, and hatred. We have that power. We are powerful far beyond what many can imagine.

It all starts with *You*. Empower yourself. Yes, be self-ish. *Self*-ish is a good thing. It's a very good thing to take care of the Self. This is a necessity. It is essential. You must empower *yourself* first. Each of us has that responsibility. And if each of us found the courage to take that responsibility, we of course would see great changes in the world. Become a Peaceful Warrior. Live a life of love and peace and make your presence known.

Remember:

> *To change the world*
>
> *around us, we must first*
>
> *change the world within us.*

# We Are One
## or
## Are We?

* * *

When we take a look around us, we see over 10,000 separate religions and belief systems in the world. There are over 100 different political parties in the United States alone. We block our countries off from each other. We've been fighting and killing each other since the beginning of time. Then there's racism, sexism, and so on.

It would be easier to believe that we are all separate. And it seems that we continue to find more and more ways to separate ourselves from each other every day.

Why do we do this?

Basically, because we've come to this planet to create the *Illusion of Separateness.* Our spiritual energy
has created these physical bodies to have the experience of being different—just one of an infinite
amount of experiences our spirits are capable of
creating. Many of us, however, have started to accept
this illusion as our only reality.

The other reality is that once we leave our bodies
behind, we are absolutely all ONE. We are one and
the same with all the beautiful energy of love and
light in the Universe. In this pure form there is no
judgment, no right or wrong, no good or bad. It is
only in these physical forms that we indulge ourselves in these illusions of being different.

Once we leave our bodies behind, our Grand Intelligent energy flows on, doing whatever it wants to
do, wherever and whenever it wants to do it, taking
on whatever form it desires. There are no restrictions. There is no time. There is only *immense joy*
and *bliss.* **Pure love.** This energy is always changing,
always evolving. It is ONE with the entire Universe
and everything in it and beyond. And of course, this
energy is YOU.

Okay, now let's come back down to Earth. So, here
we are in human form, just another creation of our
energy. Our spirit is now having an Earth Plane

experience, a *physical experience.* It can FEEL. It can feel love, pleasure, pain, anger, a whole range of sensations and emotions.

These are all wonderful illusions. But, we have become very lost in these illusions. We have forgotten how to re-connect to our spiritual energies. We're running around confused, weak and insecure, not remembering that we are just an illusion or manifestation of spiritual intelligence. And we've been creating rules and laws that go completely against our true spiritual nature.

We've become so attached to our physical selves that we have even created an illusion we call *death.* Many of us fear this illusion more than any other, and so much so that we stop enjoying life in the moment because we're thinking about how it might end.

To our spirit, however, there is no such thing as death. No beginning and no end. Just one experience and then another. We're here in one form, and then we're there in another form. Our energy has been doing this from the beginning of time. Once we understand this, we will understand the joy of living in each moment. This is *Enlightenment.*

Throughout history, there have been those who have re-connected to their higher self; those who

have learned to fully enjoy this experience knowing that it's all a wonderful illusion. And they have
tried their very best to help others to understand it
as well.

Some have listened to these enlightened beings'
teachings and have awakened. The majority, sadly,
have not. They have misunderstood and misinter-
preted these teachings.

Not being able to grasp the fact that they themselves
are this powerful, universal, spiritual energy, they
often view the enlightened teachers as Supreme
Beings. They then go on to worship these teachers
or masters, rather than become what the masters
had intended them to become in the first place.
This behavior of following, of course, doesn't serve
to empower anyone. Quite the opposite. To follow
is to give up one's power.

To further complicate things, many of these masters start to enjoy controlling and manipulating
those who easily and willingly give up their power
to follow.

Many of the most famous modern gurus continue
this practice. They speak beautiful words while they
have impressionable young people sitting at their
feet like puppy dogs.

It takes a truly enlightened master not to get caught up in their own ego and power over others. But, this is also part of the physical experience.

Everything in life is a choice. There will always be those who choose to follow and there will always be those who choose to take advantage of them.

Now, many of my 'spiritual' friends go on and on about being one with each other and bringing everyone together on this planet. But, all they seem to do is create more and more groups, which of course causes more separation. I must get hundreds of requests a week to join various groups that are going to change the world.

But, every group must have leaders. And when there are leaders, there must be followers. And then there are rules. And then there will be some who disagree, so they go and start their own group.

I say, "Enough with the groups already!" As the great comedian, Groucho Marx, once said, "I will never be a part of any group that would have me as a member."

So, here is my solution for ONENESS on this planet:

➤ First, leave every religion or group you belong to that has rules, regulations, restrictions, laws, and labels—any expectations.

➢ Next, spend time on and with yourself. Yes, be *selfish*. Remember, you cannot truly be ONE with anyone else until you've truly learned to be ONE with yourself.

You cannot *truly love* anyone until you've learned how to *truly love* yourself.

As each of us learns how to fully connect to our spiritual energy or spiritual source, we will automatically become *one* with each other.

When you connect to Source you are connected to all the energy in the Universe.

You must first *detach* yourselves from the physical illusions. You must recognize yourself as God. When you can do this, you will recognize everyone else as God. Then and only then will you fully be able to enjoy and accept each other as One.

We would then, in fact, be one large ...

### *Group~less Group*

This would be just ONE planet of Earth Beings, all loving and enjoying each other's differences. There's no need to join a group that you are automatically a part of.

Imagine each person on the planet devoted to loving themselves. What would happen? Their love would constantly overflow to everyone else.

We wouldn't need to go to church or temple to be together. The world would be our place of worship. The beaches, the mountains, and the forests would be where we meet others to share our lives. No matter where you traveled, you would find others who are filled with love, peace, happiness, and joy.

Families of complete strangers would greet each other in any of these places and embrace and laugh and enjoy each other fully. Can you live this way? I do. And I hope one day you'll join me.

### *ONENESS*

*The Powers of the Universe, or whatever you wish to call them, are always **within us**, **around us**, and **of us**.*

*In our physical forms, however, we have learned much neediness, dependence, fear, and so on. We have strayed far from understanding the Connection to Spirit or the meaning of Oneness.*

*We must **Separate** or **Detach** from these physical manifestations to break the chains of dysfunction and to fully understand the Power of the Source from which we all* *came. We must, in essence, learn how to be **alone** so we can learn how to **BE** with others on the healthiest level.*

*To walk alone is to have no need of anyone to fulfill you or make you whole or complete. It is to **understand your own Truth** and create your own paths in life, rather than blindly following other people, groups, dogmas, or doctrines.*

*It is **SELF-EMPOWERMENT**.*

*This is the Great Paradox. To be alone is to understand our connection with each other and with the POWERS of the Universe.*

*So, it is actually **detachment** or **separation** that allows us to truly **BE ONE**.*

# *Who are You?*

***

You are a *grand and glorious* spirit.

You are *light and love.*

You are the *essence of the Universe.*

You are a *power* that flows endlessly through time and space.

You are a *traveler* on a never ending journey of infinite experiences.

You are forever *evolving.*

You are forever *changing.*

You are *wonder* and *excitement.*

You exist here and at the farthest reaches of the Cosmos.

You are the *past,* the *present,* and the *future.* You are a *marvelous, mystical,* and a *magical force.*

But ... in this micro measure of time, in this physical manifestation we call 'human,' you, like most of us, have **forgotten** this.

Many will continue to walk the same old path. Many will continue to see themselves as finite beings with a beginning and an end.

Many will continue to get caught up in all the man-made dramas.

Many will continue to experience anger, fear, and frustrations.

But ... you can start to take a different view of the world and yourself right now. ***The choice is yours****.* The choice has always been yours.

You can start to see all the judgments, labels, groups, religions, and so on for what they are: false belief systems.

You can *release* the fears and insecurities that you've been holding onto.

You can dig deep and *find the courage* to open your eyes.

You can *come out* from under the covers and *see the light*.

You can move forward with *ease* and confidence.

You can *empower* yourself.

You can be *free*.

You can find a *truth* that will lift you higher than you've ever been lifted before.

> *You are the Grand, Magnificent Creator of your Life.*
> *You are the Power you've been searching for.*
> *You are God.*

# Part 2

\* \* \*

# Streams
## of
## Consciousness

\* \* \*

Here you'll find a magical grab bag of well over 200 mini thoughts or bursts of inspiration. I've always loved the challenge of putting a big thought into a little package. So enjoy these little packages about *Life, Love, Relationships, Sex, God, Religion, Spirituality, Enlightenment, Happiness, Self-empowerment,* and more.

Whether you agree, disagree, laugh or groan; whether they make you happy or angry; I hope somehow that they inspire you to think about yourself and life differently.

Have fun! And always remember ... the answers you seek are already within you. I hope that these are all just wonderful **Reminders**.

### *How to use the Streams of Consciousness*

*You may choose to close your eyes, flick open a page, and point with your finger. And there you have your message for the day!*

*Or if you're looking for something specific—Religion, God, Love or Sex, for example—you can travel to the INDEX of quotes on page 189. There you will find many 'Keywords' to choose from. The numbers listed beside the keywords refer to the number of each <u>quote</u>, NOT the page number.*

(1)

I follow no religion, but I love religiously. I don't embrace
'a' God, yet I'm guided by the godliness within me. I'm
deeply connected to my Infinite Source, one with the Powers of Universe and one with every glorious being. This
is MY experience. It's Pure, Natural, Beautiful, Freeing,
Peaceful, Empowering, and Enlightening. It's Simple. It's
LOVE. Welcome to My World.

\* \* \*

(2)

The Universe is not set up to grant wishes. It is set up to
match your level of belief.

\* \* \*

(3)

Always Know and Believe that you deserve the BEST.
The Universe will start to comply.

\* \* \*

(4)

The Universe does not judge. It simply **responds** to what you put out. If you harm another human being, harm will come to you. Not because the Universe is punishing you, but because you are vibrating with a certain Energy, and the Universe will simply return that Energy to you. Fortunately, the same thing applies to Love and Kindness. That's how perfect it is.

\* \* \*

(5)

You **won't** find me sitting in a church or temple, following ancient rituals and ideas. You **will** find me, however, on a beach or mountain, in a forest or park, or at a lake, deeply connecting to nature in all its Divine Glory. No Walls, No Roof (Metaphorically and Literally). This is where **Energy flows,** beautifully and freely. This is where I **connect** wholly and completely to my True Nature, my Divine Source.

\* \* \*

(6)

I LOVE myself and others Wholly, Passionately, and Deeply. I'm Kind and Generous. I'm devoted to the well-being of everyone on this planet. I'm devoted to world peace. I'm incredibly grateful to the powers of the Universe. Yet, I follow NO ONE. I have NO guru. NO religion. I'm NOT a member of any organized belief system. What does this make me? ... Very happy and very spiritual!

\* \* \*

(7)

Enlightened beings do not condemn others for having different beliefs. Enlightened beings do not threaten others with eternal suffering. Enlightened beings understand that those who do are the ones who live in fear and darkness. Enlightened beings know that the Power is **within us**, NOT looking down on us. Enlightened beings know we are **All One** and simply live as examples of Love and Light.

\* \* \*

(8)

If you have been taught to Fear the Universe, if you
believe in a Universe that controls you, punishes, or
rewards you, you will never connect to or understand its
True Grand Powers. Know that the
Universe is within you. The Power is YOURS.
The Power is YOU.

\* \* \*

(9)

When one is filled with anger, he will create a God who
is wrathful. When one is filled with fear, he will create a
God who imposes his will and punishes those who don't
follow. When one becomes Fully Enlightened, he will have
no need to create a God at all for he will only see the Godliness within himself.

\* \* \*

(10)

What religion are you? What political affiliation are you?
What demographic category are you in? What psycho-

logical profile are you? To LABEL yourself is to LIMIT yourself. Your mind and spirit are **boundless, unlimited,** and **infinite**. Perhaps it's time to set them FREE.

\* \* \*

(11)

There are those who find comfort in the thought that some-one or something 'out there' is in control of their lives or destiny. Then there are those of us who have stepped outside the comfort zone and feel **empowered** by the thought that WE are in control of our Lives.

\* \* \*

(12)

When you connect to your Higher Power, you are simply allowing yourself to unlock the answers that are already there. You are not separate from the Universe. You are ONE with these great powers. These energies don't sit and look down on you. They are IN you. They are AROUND you. They are OF you.

\* \* \*

(13)

Many say that SEEING is Believing. I like to say that
BELIEVING is Seeing. For what we believe most powerfully,
will certainly manifest in our Lives. Do you Believe the world
is a 'hateful place' or a 'Loving Place.' Choose your Beliefs
WISELY.

\* \* \*

(14)

Spirituality is **not** pretending that negative energy doesn't
exist. It's **balance**. It's learning to use negative energy as a
Powerful Guide for Growth and Enlightenment. When we live
a life of Love, hate does not disappear. It just becomes power-
less over us—a friendly reminder to stay on the right path.

\* \* \*

(15)

Spirituality is a Round Table. No one sits at the head
of it. Learn from everyone you meet ... But, let No One
TELL you what to think or believe. You will never find
yourself by walking someone else's path

\* \* \*

(16)

We are as Small and Insignificant as we are Grand and
Magnificent. In relation to the Universe, we are just
microscopic organisms on an infinitesimal particle of dust
floating through space. Our minds and spirits, however,
are **boundless**, reaching to the farthest corners of the Cosmos. Let your spirit soar.

\* \* \*

(17)

If you haven't found the Key to the Universe then Stop
Looking. There is NO Key. The door has ALWAYS been
Unlocked. It's your own Fears and False Beliefs that have
kept you from opening it. Fear of the unknown. Fear of
change. Fear that nothing will be as you have been lead to
Believe. Most people remain behind the door. Few have
gone out to Play in the Light. We Hope to see more of you
soon.

* * *

(18)

No one goes to Heaven or Hell. YOU Create Heaven or Hell right where you are.

* * *

(19)

No matter how far you've traveled on your journey to Enlightenment, there's always…Out There.

* * *

(20)

Lift weights to strengthen your body. Lift your thoughts to strengthen your spirit.

* * *

(21)

On our Spiritual Journey of Learning and Educating, we must accept and understand the anger that some will have toward us. Spirituality is all about making Great

Changes. Many people Fear Change. Many are involved in belief systems based on fear. And anger is just a manifestation of this fear. Never let it stand in the way of your own Spiritual Growth.

\* \* \*

(22)

Recognize that you are a MIRACLE. Then you will start to recognize all the miracles happening around you that you've been missing.

\* \* \*

(23)

Our bodies are Grand Vehicles in which our spirits can enjoy a physical experience here on Earth. Make it a pleasant one. Treat your bodies well.

\* \* \*

(24)

We each have access to the same Higher Power. Call it whatever you like: God, Universal Energy, Divine Source,

Gaia ... It exists at every level of our being and extends out to the farthest reaches of the Universe. This power is always there. You don't need to look for it or develop it. You only need to TRUST it. Just trusting a little bit will start opening the channels to allow this energy to work in your life.

\* \* \*

(25)

You may follow one of the 10,000 religions and belief systems in the world. You may follow one of the thousands of gurus and prophets. But, nowhere will you learn more about LIFE than when you Trust and Believe in yourself and follow your own Heart. The **power is within you**. It has ALWAYS been there. Try to remember.

\* \* \*

(26)

The more we connect spiritually, the more we learn to celebrate being Human. After all, that is why we're here. And Sexuality is one of the most MAGICAL WAYS to celebrate. To deny or condemn Adult Sexuality in any way goes against every Spiritual Law. What does your belief system say about Sex?

\* \* \*

(27)

Christian, Muslim, Hindu, Jew .... We ALL come from the SAME SOURCE. Let's learn in this New Age of Enlightenment that there is NO need for those LABELS which have been separating us.

\* \* \*

(28)

You don't need to know how the Universe was formed to be Mystified by its Magnificence. You don't need to know WHY you're here to be grateful and to **love yourself** for the MIRACLE that you are. FEEL the Beauty and the Joy within you and around you. Enjoy the Wonder. Enjoy the Mystery. Enjoy the Magic. Enjoy the Love. Enjoy the journey as each answer reveals itself to you.

\* \* \*

(29)

Each religion is just a different flavor of ice cream. Yours may taste delicious to you, but not to someone else. Don't force your taste on others. Your ice cream is no better, just different. Simply SAVOR and ENJOY the flavor you have chosen. Although I have tasted and enjoyed dozens of flavors, I don't care for ice cream at all. No need to convince me that I'm missing something.

I'm happy with sorbet. ♥

\* \* \*

(30)

Any belief system that instills Fear into the minds of children cannot be True. There is No Truth in Fear. Fear is a lie used to control, manipulate, and restrain their Spirits. Fear is the Darkness that prevents them from Knowing who they truly are. Children must be guided into the Light. Empower them with Self-Love, Self-Respect, and Self-Responsibility.

\* \* \*

(31)

I believe in a Powerful Universe. I believe in a Powerful YOU. I believe in a Powerful ME. I believe in the Power of LOVE and Complete Responsibility. I believe in being FREE.

\* \* \*

(32)

The Universe is not religious. When someone is drown-
ing and a person jumps in to save that person, is it religion
that motivates the action? No, it's the **divine spirit** of that
person that compels him/her to save a life. It's the natural
flow of the Universe in action. It exists in all of us. No
one group can claim it. It needs no label. It simply is. We
know it is right. It is Universal Law.

\* \* \*

(33)

You are ONE with the powers that created you. When you
put yourself down, you put down the Universe. You are
DIVINE. Treat yourself that way. **Praise yourself** for just
being alive. This is how you start connecting to your Source.

\* \* \*

(34)

We are here for the Blink of an Eye. Make it the Most
Grand Experience imaginable. Stop searching. Stop fol-

lowing. Stop being controlled and manipulated by Archaic Thoughts and Superstitions. The Greatest Powers of the Universe are within you. Be Free. Empower yourself. Live your life to the fullest. You are Magnificent.

\* \* \*

(35)

Look around you ... the Sky, the Stars, the Mountains, the Forests, the Oceans ... The same energy that exists in them exists in YOU. Be in awe of everything around you and you will understand YOUR OWN GREATNESS.

\* \* \*

(36)

The Universe had its own laws long before man created his laws and religions. But, the more we lost our connection to the natural laws of the Universe, the more we relied on the laws written down by men. Unfortunately, many of these men have been ruled by their ego, not their spirit. Therefore, man has turned many of these religious laws into ways of controlling the masses and taking away freedom.

\* \* \*

(37)

The Universe is perfect. Its laws are perfect. When you
flow with them your life works on every level. Joy and
happiness become your way of life. When you go against
them, life becomes an uphill battle of guilt, confusion,
anger, and frustration. Let your emotions be your guide.

\* \* \*

(38)

All of our problems on Earth stem from one thing: we have
become disconnected from our higher power. Thus, the
mind becomes consumed only with the physical experience. When the mind is deeply connected to the Spiritual
Energies, it is divinely guided. It is only concerned with
manifesting Joy, Health, Happiness, and Well-being.
When we lose the Spiritual Connection, the ego takes
over. Feelings of Lack, Insecurity, Envy, Jealousy, Hatred,
and Anger become more common.

\* \* \*

(39)

There can be Great Joy in NOT knowing. It is the Mysteries of the Universe that keep the Flames of Excitement burning. How wonderful, at times, to be a Bright Eyed Child. Live, Love, Laugh, and Smile with surprise and amazement.

\* \* \*

(40)

There really is a Magic Lamp. It is NOT buried in some far off cave, however, but buried deep within your own minds, under levels of Misunderstandings, Misinterpretations, and Mistaken beliefs. This adventure begins by UNPACKING. The more of these antiquated thoughts you release, the quicker you'll find the Treasure. The Magic Awaits. Have a Glorious Journey.

\* \* \*

(41)

We choose our lives before we get here. We choose our family, location in the world, environment, and so on. And though some may come here to face great challenges, it doesn't make them helpless victims. This doesn't mean we don't Feel for or Help those through these challenges. These LESSONS are for ALL of us to learn. Show Compassion, not Distress. Empower others, Don't Pity them.

\* \* \*

(42)

Next time you take a walk, Notice if you're looking down at the ground or if your head is held high to view All the Beauty above and around you. This little adjustment can change your Energy drastically. Open up your Field of Awareness and let your Spirit soar.

\* \* \*

(43)

We humans are a superstitious lot. We create many ways to stifle and restrict ourselves. We look for meaning in symbols, signs, numbers, prophecies, folk lore, religions, and so on. But, **true meaning** comes only by searching within our own hearts or spirit. Once we understand this, once we start to **awaken**, all else fades away. It's time for **change**. It's time to **let go**. It's time to GROW.

\* \* \*

(44)

To be Enlightened and filled with Love is to accept all religions and belief systems. Yet, not one religion truly accepts another. They must, by their very nature, disagree and/or oppose the others. You cannot tell a person that you love them unconditionally and in the next breath tell them they will suffer eternally if they don't follow your belief. This is hypocrisy.

\* \* \*

(45)

The Universe does not hold one religion above another. Your religion may be the one for you, but it is **not THE One**. In fact, to understand Universal Law is to see NO USE for religion at all. We don't even necessarily see Right and Wrong. We understand, however, that there are ALWAYS consequences to our actions. The energy you put out toward others will SURELY come back to you. This is YOUR choice.

\* \* \*

(46)

You are not separate from the Universe. You are one with it and its Great Powers. These energies don't sit and look down on you. They are in you. They are of you. This energy flows as freely as the air you breathe. Start to imagine Love, Health, and Happiness flowing through you with every breath. Imagine every cell of your body being charged with this Positive, Powerful Energy. You are connected to a never ending source of Divine Power.

\* \* \*

(47)

We are one with this planet and everyone in it. Each one of us affects everyone else. We are all of the same Energy. Love, Health, Happiness, Wealth, Success, Prosperity, Peace, and Joy are entirely our choice. We need only to take a few moments each day to be grateful and allow this energy to flow. This energy is always here. It is this energy that attracted us to this planet. It is this energy that created us. It is this energy that will carry us into the next level.

\* \* \*

(48)

I'm often confronted with, "How can you talk Love and Peace when people in the world are starving, being brutally killed, and are financially devastated?" When someone has an illness or disease, I Help them to FOCUS all their Energy on HEALING, **not** to focus on the disease. I am Ultra-Aware of Worldwide Suffering. I choose, however, to FOCUS on what will HEAL the planet, not harm it. Love and Peace.

\* \* \*

(49)

If you look to others to Fulfill you, you will Never be Fulfilled. If your Happiness depends on money, you will never know True Wealth. If you have **not** found Peace within your own mind, you cannot expect Peace in the World. All Happiness, All Joy, All Wealth, All Peace are the results of LOVING YOURSELF.

\* \* \*

(50)

Life is NOT about waiting for the right moment. It's about Creating the right moment.

* * *

(51)

Once you take Complete Responsibility for your life, there will be NO MORE EXCUSES. Every time you come up with an excuse in life, you miss an opportunity to Learn and Grow.

* * *

(52)

Most of us view Death as a Loss of Life. In reality, Death is a Continuation of Life. It is only HERE, in this reality, that we experience a true loss of life. It occurs every time we choose Fear and Anger over Love and Compassion.

* * *

(53)

Every thought, every feeling, and every action that you
take becomes an energy that directly affects what you
attract into your life. The Universe is that perfect. Choose
to flow with it or against it.

\* \* \*

(54)

You cannot make any changes in your Life until you
accept yourself at the moment. You may NOT LIKE who
you are at the moment, but you MUST ACCEPT it. To
accept yourself is to take Responsibility. To take responsibility is to experience complete Self-Empowerment.

\* \* \*

(55)

No matter how old you are or what you've
been through, DEVOTE the rest of your life to
LOVING YOURSELF. Leave the past behind.
With each new day you are given a NEW Chance
for a Fresh Start. Take Deep Breaths and Fill
Yourself with all the Abundance that the

Universe freely offers. It is NEVER too late to
turn your life around. It is NEVER too late
to experience JOY.

\* \* \*

(56)

No science, no philosophy, and no religion can teach you
the meaning of life, for only you can give your life meaning.

\* \* \*

(57)

If you could step outside of yourself and become your own
Life Coach, what would you do? Be Angry with yourself
or be Comforting? Say how Beautiful you are or point
out Flaws? Tell yourself that you can have Anything
you Desire, or say that Life is just Too Tough? Say you
are Always Loved and Cherished or you're Not Good
Enough? It's time to realize that the most Powerful Life
Coach lives in your own Heart.

\* \* \*

(58)

CHANGE in your Life is inevitable. HOW you change,
however, is entirely your responsibility.

\* \* \*

(59)

If there is No Life after death and this is all we get, then
nothing really matters and we should just enjoy every minute that we're here. On the other hand, if we do actually
get to come back and learn unfinished lessons, then nothing really matters and we should just enjoy every minute
that we're here. So my advice is: Enjoy every minute that
you're here.

\* \* \*

(60)

Your Life is Sacred. Your Spirit is Sacred. Your
Love is Sacred. You don't NEED anyone in your
life who doesn't appreciate this. You don't need
to do anything, create anything, or be anything

for anyone. The day you understand your own
GREATNESS is the day your life will start working
for you on every level. Above all else, Love Yourself ~
Be Free and Powerful.

\* \* \*

(61)

Life is all about Choice. Choose a bumper sticker: 'Shit
Happens' or 'Magic Happens.' It's all about how you
wish to see the World. To those of us who understand our
Thoughts are Powerful Tools that Shape our Destiny,
only one choice makes sense.

\* \* \*

(62)

Life is an ongoing education: a series of wonderful, valuable and sometimes challenging Lessons to be learned. So,
if your inner child doesn't like school, try to think of it as a
long field trip. You may fall in the mud, but you'll also see
some Butterflies.

\* \* \*

(63)

EVERYTHING in Life is a Lesson. And I will be the
first to admit, there have been days when my inner child
just didn't want to go to school.

\* \* \*

(64)

Feed yourself unhealthy foods and your body will break
down and get sick. Feed yourself unhealthy thoughts and
the same will happen to your mind. Your mind is the most
powerful tool you have to change your life. Nourish yourself with Positive Words and Thoughts.

\* \* \*

(65)

When We're Born ~ Life is Simple and
Beautiful.

As we Learn and Grow ~ Life is Fun, Scary, Exciting,
Sad, Happy, Loving, Hateful, Confusing, Joyful, and
sometimes Overwhelming.

When Enlightened ~ Life is Simple and
Beautiful

\* \* \*

(66)

Life is filled with opportunities. You are never punished
for missing one. The Universe is abundant. For every door
that closes another one opens. You always hear about
someone who was in the right place at the right time. This
is no accident. It's your mind and spirit connecting on the
highest level.

\* \* \*

(67)

Remember that whatever you give power to will manifest
as positive or negative. If you continue to dwell on what
you don't have, you simply create more lack in your life. If
your mind is blocked with thoughts of lack and limitations
you are closing off all channels that draw in wealth and
prosperity.

\* \* \*

(68)


Never set out to change others. Rather, be an example of
Love and Kindness and let others be drawn to you.


\* \* \*

(69)


When You Fill Yourself with LOVE and GRATITUDE,
you'll SEE Everything and Everyone in the World, each
and every day, as though you were seeing them for the first
time. This is Genuine Excitement. This is Pure Joy. This
is True Happiness. This is Enlightenment

(70)


We are Born to LOVE. We Learn to Fear.
Sometimes Enlightenment is more about
UN-learning than Learning. All your Fears
are FALSE Beliefs. Remember the TRUTH.
Remember the LOVE.


\* \* \*

(71)

LOVE gives us Magical Strength. It allows us to LIFT
each other at the same time.

\* \* \*

(72)

To have a Healthy Love Relationship with another,
you must first Detach yourself from the Desire to have
one at all. You must be Perfectly Happy to be Alone
before you can be Perfectly Happy to be with
someone else.

\* \* \*

(73)

## The TRUTH.

When someone needs Help, give them a Hand.
When someone is filled with Fear, offer them
Assurance. When someone is filled with Doubt,
Praise them. When someone is Lost, offer them

Guidance. When someone is Sad, offer them Understanding. This is why we're here. This is Caring. This is Kindness. THIS IS LOVE, the ONE TRUTH that we can all agree on.

\* \* \*

(74)

LOVE is The Most Magical and Powerful Force that exists. And every single one of us has access to it. Every single one of us has The Power to Change our Lives and the World we live in. Feel the Power of LOVE. Be the Power of LOVE. USE the Power of LOVE to Help, Heal, and Enlighten.

\* \* \*

(75)

Love cannot be learned from books or teachers. Love is not an action or an achievement. Love is not a word we speak. Love is a Discovery within oneself.

\* \* \*

(76)

When you feel Hurt, Fear, or Loneliness, LOVE has not abandoned you. You have abandoned LOVE ... for these are false beliefs, and LOVE is real. Sit in Silence and Listen to the Wisdom of your HEART. SEE how quickly **love fills and surrounds you.** See how quickly these False Beliefs dissolve. I wish you all an Abundance of LOVE that fills every part of your being to the farthest reaches of the Universe.

\* \* \*

(77)

Gratitude is the magical key that unlocks the door to the most Grand Power in the Universe, Love.

\* \* \*

(78)

Loving others to receive Love is a lack of Self-worth. When you have Self-worth you are able to give Love Endlessly ... with no expectations of receiving anything back. This is the Ultimate Wealth.

\* \* \*

(79)


Searching for the meaning of Life is a journey of endless
questions. Living Life is the answer.


\* \* \*

(80)


We search and search for Love, Happiness, and Peace of
Mind. We look for answers in addictions, religions, even
other people, hoping to fill our
emptiness. In essence, we are constantly
Running Away from Ourselves. But the Answers
are Here within us. They have always been
here. When you finally stop running, you will
Find Yourself and The Truth.


\* \* \*

(81)


There is no limit to how much you can Love.
But, I highly recommend you keep trying to
reach it.


\* \* \*

(82)

SELF-LOVE needs no one else for it to Grow and Flourish. Nor can anyone change, damage, or manipulate it. It is Powerful, Passionate, Confident, and Courageous. It is Beauty, Truth, and Freedom. This is REAL LOVE. This is the Gift the World will receive only after you give it to Yourself.

\* \* \*

(83)

Each time you Hate another, you Love yourself less.

\* \* \*

(84)

When it comes to Love, two halves **Do Not** make a whole. True Love will develop only when Two Whole and Complete individuals meet. You must Fully Love Yourself before you love another.

\* \* \*

(85)


Books that teach one how to 'win' at Love or how to 'get'
a man or woman are worthless. Love is not a game. If you
try to attain it through control or manipulation; if you
think of it as something to win or lose; you will never, ever
experience its true essence. Love Fully. Never hold back.
Love with Every Part of your Being. Why would you want
to be with anyone who gives any less?

\* \* \*

(86)


When our hearts are filled with Love, the smallest living space becomes a palace; the smallest meal becomes a
feast.

\* \* \*

(87)


We need to spend more time learning to Love ourselves
than we do seeking the Love of others.

\* \* \*

(88)

There is **no excuse for mediocre sex** in a relationship
or marriage. Both partners have equal responsibility to
teach each other to fulfill all fantasies and desires. Never
assume that someone knows what to do. If there is no
communication there is no relationship. Like everything
else in life, great sex is a choice.

\* \* \*

(89)

It is true that we should LOVE Everyone— even those
who challenge or try to hurt us. However, Spirituality is
as much about Loving and Helping others as it is about
Knowing when to RELEASE Negative People and
Energy from our lives. Feel NO guilt about moving away
from people or situations that hinder your growth. Yes,
you can RELEASE them WITH LOVE.

\* \* \*

(90)

What is to be said about a society that lets their children watch gory, bloody, brutal, sadistic, violent action/horror films, but believes they will be harmed by the sight of a woman's breast?

\* \* \*

(91)

Love is one of the most misused, abused, and misunderstood feelings. It is too often confused with addiction, manipulation, control, neediness and other dysfunctional behaviors. These are the things we must learn to overcome to fully understand, appreciate, and experience Love in all its' Glory. True LOVE is always and only Warm, Embracing, Nurturing, Healing and Magical.

\* \* \*

(92)

Detachment is certainly one of the more difficult concepts for people to understand, especially when it comes to LOVE Relationships.

A Love Relationship is a grand Paradox. To have a
Healthy one, you must first Detach yourself
from the desire to have one. You must first be
perfectly happy to be alone before you can be
perfectly happy with another.

\* \* \*

(93)

Love comes to those who Love themselves.

\* \* \*

(94)

How many still believe this: "You always hurt the one
you Love"? Well, that would be impossible. If you hurt
someone mentally or physically, it's a LACK of Love and
respect for that person and yourself. Please understand
this. Any Hurt is Abuse ~ NOT Love. If you are abused
and told that you're loved afterward...Get Out and/or
seek help. Where there is Love there is Only Happiness
and Joy.

\* \* \*

(95)

Falling in love is a fantasy inspired by romance novels and
Hollywood movies. Love takes time. Find someone to LIKE
and plant the seed. Have patience. If Love grows, the roots
will be deep and the fruit incredibly sweet.

\* \* \*

(96)

Sometimes the greatest expression of love in a
relationship is recognizing when it is not
working and RELEASING each other with
all the BEST WISHES.

\* \* \*

(97)

When you can look into a mirror and say, "I Love You"
with absolute conviction, others will see the same reflection in your eyes.

\* \* \*

(98)

Those who worry about being hurt
can never love completely.

\* \* \*

(99)

When your Heart is filled with Love and Joy, a bird, a tree,
a blue sky ... the stars you've seen a thousand times ... will
take your breath away.

\* \* \*

(100)

Love is a magical, powerful emotion that must be
expressed from your Heart with tenderness and affection.
Just saying you love someone without the emotion is like
giving a gift box without the present.

\* \* \*

(101)

The Paradox of the Heart ~ When it's Empty it's Heavy.
The more it Fills with Love, the Lighter it gets.

\* \* \*

(102)

There is nothing more beautiful than people who Love
themselves. There is nothing more unattractive than
people who are 'in love' with themselves.

\* \* \*

(103)

SELF-LOVE is the basis for All Love. It starts with
YOU.

\* \* \*

(104)

When the Heart is filled with Need, we 'Fall' in Love.
When the Heart is filled with Joy, we 'Flow' with Love.

\* \* \*

(105)

You may find yourself alone at times. But, if you truly
Love Yourself you will never feel lonely.

\* \* \*

(106)

Men project toughness and strength because it hides their
fragility. Women tend to project fragility because it hides
their inner power that, unfortunately, is frightening to
most men.

(107)

We often seek others who will love us. We seek
Relationships, Groups and so on. But, our Hearts will
always remain empty until we learn to Love ourselves.
You cannot Seek Love. You can only
Become LOVE.

\* \* \*

(108)

Gazing into each other's eyes makes Love Passionate.
Gazing outwardly in the same direction, makes
Love Last.

\* \* \*

(109)

A Man wonders how many relationships a woman has
had. A Woman wonders how much a man has learned
from them.

\* \* \*

(110)

Both partners have equal responsibility to
EXPRESS their Likes, Dislikes, Needs, Fantasies,
and Desires. Never assume that your partner can
read your mind. If there is no communication, there
is no relationship.

\* \* \*

(111)

The most important relationship is
the one you have with yourself.

\* \* \*

(112)

This is Your Moment!!! And so is the Next One. We
Live in a Universe of Infinite Possibilities.

\* \* \*

(113)

For thousands of years Women have been slaves to the
belief that they are the Weaker Sex. Those who have broken the shackles have come to understand that they are in
fact, The More Powerful Sex. This, of course, is frightening to any man who lacks Self-Confidence and Self-Love.
The men who embrace this will enjoy a much more powerful Life Experience.

\* \* \*

(114)

Relationships are manifestations of your innermost
thoughts and feelings, positive or negative. The person
that you attract will Always match your own level of
Health or Dysfunction. If you are unhappy in a relationship there are two questions to ask: What is it within
yourself that has attracted this person, and why are you
still there? Remember, the challenge is not attracting
someone in your life, it's attracting someone healthy.

\* \* \*

(115)

As long as a woman allows herself to feel
inferior around a man, she will encourage
his arrogance.

\* \* \*

(116)

The Universe has blessed women with much power.
Throughout history, men have created many ways to prevent them from using it.

\* \* \*

(117)

Most of us have been raised to feel that we cannot be
complete without a partner. Nothing could be further from
the truth. No one can or will ever complete you. And no
one ever should. You are the only one who can Complete
Yourself.

\* \* \*

(118)

A great marriage is like owning a new car. You shouldn't
have to work on it all the time. Just make sure it gets a
periodic tune up

\* \* \*

(119)

Healthy Relationships need to be supported by two pillars
of Equal Strength. The weakness of one will cause the
collapse of both. Each should be devoted to the Strength of
the other.

\* \* \*

(120)

A Healthy Relationship seeks communication with each
other through the most challenging times.
An Unhealthy Relationship seeks friends to
complain to.

\* \* \*

(121)

There is no war between men and women. Only a war
within Yourself. If you truly Love yourself, if you truly
respect yourself, you will have Love and Respect for anyone you're in a relationship with.

\* \* \*

(122)

The Sun does **not teach** us about Light and Warmth.
We are DRAWN to its Radiance and we ABSORB it.
The Ocean does not teach us about its Flowing Energy.
We OBSERVE it and FEEL its Power. A Rainbow does
not teach us about Beauty. We GAZE at it and we're

inspired. ... We Cannot teach anyone about LOVE. We can only BECOME LOVE and allow others to Experience our Joy.

\* \* \*

(123)

Telling others you Love them to obtain their Love is a lack of Self-Worth. When you have Self-Worth you are able to give Love Endlessly with no expectation of receiving anything back. This is Ultimate WEALTH.

\* \* \*

(124)

When you can look in a mirror and say, "I Love You," with absolute conviction, others will see the same reflection in your eyes.

\* \* \*

(125)

To truly know Love and Happiness, you must
first fully accept yourself on every level. All is
Perfect when we learn to accept our
Imperfections.

\* \* \*

(126)

Why is it that when someone finally gets what they
wanted, the first thing they say is, "I don't believe it!" ...
BELIEVE it ... or it probably won't happen again.

\* \* \*

(127)

Choose your thoughts Wisely. If you tell your mind
anything for long enough it will not only Believe it, it will
MANIFEST it. Good or Bad. There is nothing wrong
with believing you CAN have everything in life you
desire. There is something wrong with believing you can't.
Plant the seeds of belief and watch it grow.

\* \* \*

(128)

Who you are, where you are, what you think, and how you feel is YOUR CHOICE. Everything in your life can be changed if you understand this.

\* \* \*

(129)

If you are in a place of Darkness and Despair, I want you to think about one thing. You are as much a Beautiful Creation of Life as any magnificent thing on this planet. No matter what you look like or feel like, no matter what challenges you're facing, the energy that created you is the same energy that created everything around you. You are Divine

\* \* \*

(130)

I often hear the expression, 'Push Beyond Yourself.' The truth is most people are not even close to Knowing themselves. I say just 'Learn to Become Yourself.' You cannot be greater than who you truly are. And who you Truly are is Magnificent.

\* \* \*

(131)

NEVER put Yourself Down for not reaching a goal. It's REACHING for the goal that has Pushed you Further Ahead. Turn your Disappointment into PRAISE. Reach for the stars so you may Touch the Sky.

\* \* \*

(132)

To Know Yourself is to Attain Ultimate WEALTH. But first, you must overcome your Fears. Remember, The GREATEST TREASURE lies behind every door that you FEAR to open.

\* \* \*

(133)

Most of you have been taught that SELFISH is Bad. How could that possibly be True? The Self is who you are. You are here to Learn about Your-Self. You Cannot KNOW Others until You Know Your-Self. You Cannot GIVE completely to others until you've given completely To Your-Self. Always Be SELFISH First. The more you give to YOU, the more YOU have to GIVE.

This is truly how you strengthen your SPIRIT and those
around you.

\* \* \*

(134)

Those who control and manipulate others are NOT
Powerful at all. They're actually Weak and Fearful. They
fill their Egos with a False Sense of Superiority by Preying
on those who easily give up their own power. Remember,
NO ONE can Take Your Power unless YOU give it.
And when You are Truly Empowered, you will NEVER
allow that to happen. Know Yourself. Love and Trust
Yourself. Empower Yourself.

\* \* \*

(135)

I AM RESPONSIBLE—three of the most Powerful
Words you can learn. WE ~ create seemingly overwhelm-
ing challenges to teach ourselves Strength and Self-
Empowerment. WE ~ create dysfunctional relationships
to teach ourselves how to Love. When we learn to take
Complete Responsibility for the situations in our lives,

the Universe rewards us with the Greatest Gifts of all ~
TRUST and FAITH in Ourselves.

\* \* \*

(136)

How many of you use this expression: "It's too good to be
true."? This is Absolute Sabotage. This is the Quickest
Road to Failure. Eliminate this Thought as quickly as you
can from your Consciousness! The Universe wants you
to have Everything you Desire. But, you Must turn your
Powerful (Negative) Beliefs, into Powerful (POSITIVE)
Beliefs. Know, Feel, and Believe that YOU Deserve the
BEST.

\* \* \*

(137)

When you take things personally you give up All your
Power. You become a Victim. Remember, anyone who
judges you in the first place is only projecting their own
Fears, Doubts, and Insecurities. It is They who are coming from a place of Extreme Weakness. Knowing this, You
can Hold Your Head Up high and smile at them. This

not only removes the sword from their hand, but Greatly
Empowers YOUR SPIRIT.

\* \* \*

(138)

Your Thoughts and Beliefs are your Destiny. Yes, you are
that powerful. You are the Creator of the world in which
you live. When you understand this, you understand that
~ Happiness is a Choice~ Always Empower yourself
with POSITIVE thinking. The Universe WILL comply.

\* \* \*

(139)

We must Learn to make Ourselves Happy before we can
bring Happiness to the World.

\* \* \*

(140)

Be Careful. One POSITIVE thought can
change your Whole Day. Make it a
BEAUTIFUL One.

\* \* \*

(141)

I have NO Desire to foresee the future. My DESIRE is to Enjoy Each Precious Moment as it unfolds.

\* \* \*

(142)

We often confuse Forgiveness with Acceptance. When we Forgive someone we are NOT Accepting the bad behavior. We are simply Loving ourselves enough to Release the negative energy that has affected us. At this point, we can either give the 'forgiven' person another chance or simply Release them Completely with NO Attachments. Either way, we are FREE to Move On and Grow.

\* \* \*

(143)

We must be Fully Aware of the problems in the world without ingesting them. We must Feel Deeply for those going through great challenges, without becoming overwhelmed. We must Live in the Light while others try to pull us into darkness. This is the Strength, Power, Love,

and Faith that it takes to lift others and make positive
changes in the world.

\* \* \*

(144)

There is no great secret to Happiness. You must just
Believe that you Deserve it.

\* \* \*

(145)

True FREEDOM comes from controlling our own minds,
not by letting groups or other individuals control them.

\* \* \*

(146)

Identify your Fears. Explore them. Understand them.
These are the True Treasure Troves of Self-Knowledge.

\* \* \*

(147)

You Cannot give this Gift to anyone. Nor can you
Receive this Gift from anyone. This is a gift you can only
Give to Yourself. That gift is PEACE of MIND—a
Grand, Glorious, and Powerful Gift. Please, Be Very
Generous to Yourself.

\* \* \*

(148)

Some say, "You shouldn't be too honest." For me, there's
no such thing as being too honest. You're Honest or you're
Not. There's only One Rule I abide by: 'Never volunteer
an opinion.' My Friendship comes with One Warning: Ask
what I think and you will get a completely Honest, Uned-
ited, Uncensored response. I'd rather have only One Friend
in my life who can deal with it than many with whom I must
tiptoe around.

\* \* \*

(149)

To Accept who you are and where you are, does not
mean you are resigned to stay that way.

Self-Acceptance is taking complete responsibility for your actions and consequences, which gives you the awareness and power to change.

\* \* \*

(150)

Those who understand their own Greatness are willing to Bow the Lowest.

\* \* \*

(151)

We can only do the best we know how at any given moment. So, no matter what the outcome, always Praise Yourself for Trying.

\* \* \*

(152)

When you find yourself Angered about certain concepts, such as Self-Healing, Manifesting Wealth, or Manifesting Happiness, then it is very important to examine where that Anger comes from. Here is where you will find

exactly what has been holding you back from achieving
these things.

\* \* \*

(153)

Only Believe your own Experience. Believe what you Know
and Feel. Don't put anyone on a higher pedestal than yourself. To learn from another you must look into their eyes.
Know your Power. Feel your Power. Believe in your Power.
No One is Greater than You.

\* \* \*

(154)

As soon as you Trust Yourself, you will Know how to Live.

\* \* \*

(155)

Try hard NOT to resist Life Lessons, but to Flow with
them. We are not hit so hard by the waves when we learn
to ride them.

\* \* \*

(156)

Art should not be Judged. It's an individual expression.
You enjoy it or you don't. You are All Works of Art. Let
No One Judge you.

\* \* \*

(157)

We have all met with great challenges from time to time.
Of course, the real Lessons come, not just by getting
through them, but by recognizing WHY we created them
in the first place. For many this concept is a great challenge in and of itself. Certainly, the more we realize this,
the more we can avoid them in the future.

\* \* \*

(158)

Most of our Fears are like shadows. As soon as we shine
some Light on them, they disappear.

\* \* \*

(159)

No One learns courage from observing another. Sometimes we have to be pushed from a tree to learn to fly.

\* \* \*

(160)

The goal of a Free Thinker is not necessarily to be liked, but to challenge the thinking of others. This takes courage. Sometimes we must shake the pan to separate the silt from the Gold Dust. Don't be afraid to shake the pan from time to time.

\* \* \*

(161)

The Past can be a mental prison. The Future can be a mental Maze. There is only Freedom in the present.

\* \* \*

(162)

Be Honest with Yourself rather than Trying to Please Others. Don't concern yourself with being Loved, but with Loving Yourself and helping others learn to Love Themselves. Be prepared to walk alone and soon you will have Beautiful Company.

\* \* \*

(163)

Our Mind is Where we Live. Our Mind is How we Live. If we live in a Dark Home, we can't see all the dust that has accumulated. We must first shine Light in our home before we can start cleaning and making it a place of Beauty.

\* \* \*

(164)

There will always be more that I don't know than what I do know. True wisdom is in knowing how much you don't know. And therefore, I am content to be happily ignorant.

\* \* \*

(165)

Each of us owns a gift shop of Kindness with an endless supply. Give these gifts Freely and Often. It feeds our soul and makes us more powerful beings.

(166)

Courage is not about eliminating your fears. It's learning how to use your fears to motivate yourself.

\* \* \*

(167)

We have been taught to recognize certain physical traits as beautiful. We spend countless hours and thousands of dollars on ourselves, trying to manipulate our looks with make-up and surgery to 'fit' into impossible images. But, True Beauty cannot to be seen with the eyes. For True Beauty is Self-Love and Self-Confidence. This is the Beauty that Shines the Brightest.

\* \* \*

(168)

Every enlightened person has gained their wisdom by making mistakes. Welcome them. Embrace them. Learn from them. But, try very hard not to repeat them.

\* \* \*

(169)

The day you ask someone else how to
live your life is the day you stop living.

\* \* \*

(170)

No One can take your power unless you
give it. No One on earth can control you once
you've Empowered yourself with Courage, Discipline,
Responsibility, and Self-Respect.

(171)

Before we were taught doubt and insecurity, before we were taught fear and prejudice, we were born Absolutely Pure. We were One with Ourselves. One with the Universe. One with All. We were the very Essence of Love and Joy and Wonder. This is Who We Were. THIS IS WHO WE ARE. Find that Child and you find Your Power.

\* \* \*

(172)

Never ignore your Feelings. Explore them. Don't fight them. Don't label them. Be with them. We have chosen to be here to experience them. They are valuable lessons for spiritual growth and self-empowerment. Remember, everything we go through is for our higher good.

(173)

Negative thoughts toward others, like the Honeybee's Sting, will always harm you more than your victim. *[Fact: When a Honeybee stings its victim the abdomen is torn out and it dies instantly—a huge price to pay for anger].*

\* \* \*

(174)

Love, Kindness, Generosity, Strength, Balance, Peace,
and Self-Esteem. SUCCESS is not what you own or
what you do. It's what you find inside of you.

\* \* \*

(175)

Negative energy exists on every level of our existence. We
cannot change it. However, to those of us who embrace it
and view it in its proper perspective, it becomes a powerful
guide. We learn Strength from the weak, Kindness from
the unkind, Generosity from the selfish, Love from the
hateful, and Peace from the violent.

\* \* \*

(176)

Growing old physically is inevitable. Growing old mentally is inexcusable!

\* \* \*

(177)

The Past is for Learning, not for Living.

\* \* \*

(178)

As an experiment, a person was blindfolded. They were
told that their arm was going to be burned with a cigarette.
Instead, they were touched with an ice cube. A burn blister
actually formed where the ice cube had touched. This is the
Power of FEAR. This is the Power of the MIND. You have
the POWER and RESPONSIBILITY to change your
Thoughts. Stop Living in Fear. Take off the Blindfolds and
Live in the LIGHT.

\* \* \*

(179)

Every one of us is a Beautiful, Perfect Diamond in the
rough. How much we Sparkle and Shine, however,
depends on how much chipping and polishing we're willing
to do.

\* \* \*

(180)

We learn Great Wisdom and Self-Empowerment through failure and perseverance. We learn nothing by quitting.

\* \* \*

(181)

Dreams are Universal Seeds. The more
you plant ... the more will grow.

\* \* \*

(182)

When you learn to see your own reflection in others, you won't be so quick to judge them.

\* \* \*

(183)

Never allow others to validate you. You don't have to do anything, create anything, or be anything for anyone. You are perfect just as you are. The day you feel just great

about your own perfection is the day your life will start
working on a higher level.

\* \* \*

(184)

We are like lamps plugged into a wall. Trusting in the
powers of the Universe will flip the switch on, allowing
magical powers to flow through us.

\* \* \*

(185)

Wisdom is not just accumulated knowledge.
It's recognizing what you need to learn.

\* \* \*

(186)

You will not receive a reward for kindness. You create the
reward by providing it.

\* \* \*

(187)

Change "When I get what I want I'll be Happy" to "When I'm Happy, I'll get what I want".

(188)

There is no shame in making mistakes, only in covering them up.

\* \* \*

(189)

If you're Lonely when you're Alone, you must really dislike the person you're with.

\* \* \*

(190)

You find Anxiety when you Live in the Future. You find Depression when you Live in the Past. You find PEACE when you Live in the Present.

\* \* \*

(191)

Many of us decide that one specific thing is needed in our lives to make it perfect, such as love or money. But, when we concentrate on that one thing, we miss in that moment the Perfection of Who We Are and the Perfection of All that is around us.

\* \* \*

(192)

We are like Prisms. The same Light shines on us all. How it comes through us, however, is what makes us each incredibly Unique and Beautiful.

\* \* \*

(193)

When you Judge another, you are refusing to SEE the things that need to be changed within yourself. Judging is simply the avoidance of Self-Responsibility. However, once you have opened your own Heart, the person you have judged will be the one who offers the most Valuable Insight to your own Life.

\* \* \*

(194)

Have you ever been given this advice: "Don't get your hopes up"? ... Are you kidding me?! GET your Hopes up! Get them up HIGH! DON'T Brace yourself for Disappointment. PREPARE yourself for MIRACLES! The more you learn to do this the more you will manifest what you want. It's time to Change those Thought Patterns.

\* \* \*

(195)

Your word is the most essential part of your character. Do your words match your actions? Do you keep your promises? Do you keep your commitments? Every lie you tell, every time you deceive another, you deplete a little bit more of your own power and energy. Ultimately, you are just lying to and deceiving yourself.

\* \* \*

(196)

> The day you stop pointing your finger at
> others is the day you start learning
> about yourself.

\* \* \*

(197)

> Dreams are Adventures into the unknown. To
> follow our Dreams we must first Embrace our
> Fears. And by doing so, we've already found
> the first treasure.

\* \* \*

(198)

> What I know, is that I am here.
>
> What I can do, is allow myself to enjoy it.

\* \* \*

(199)

Never look for someone to make you happy. Rather, look for someone with whom you can share Your Own Happiness.

\* \* \*

(200)

A good cry sometimes washes the eyes so we can see more clearly.

\* \* \*

(201)

The day you accept and feel just great about your own Perfection is the day your life will start working for you on every level.

\* \* \*

(202)

There are over 70 TRILLION CELLS in our bodies! Each individual Cell is a Fantastic Receiver and Transmitter. Each and Every Cell is directly affected by our Own

Energy or Thoughts. This is the ENERGY that will Manifest your Life Experience. You have the POWER to change your THOUGHTS and your LIFE. Learn to LOVE, ACCEPT, and APPRECIATE who you are.

\* \* \*

(203)

As EACH and every one of your 70 trillion microscopic cells holds ALL the information of the entire Body, so do you hold ALL the information of the Universe. Every Spirit is a Beautiful, Integral part of the Whole. We are ONE with the Universe. We are ONE with each other.

\* \* \*

(204)

Over thousands of lifetimes, we have programmed ourselves to think Weak, Helpless, Limited thoughts. So, it's not surprising that we live in a world of War, Poverty, and Sickness. We continue to manifest age old FALSE beliefs. It is time to stop fighting our TRUE NATURE. NOW is the Time to start thinking of ourselves as Strong, Pure, Perfect, Free, Empowered SPIRITS—the way the Universe intended.

\* \* \*

(205)

Every person I meet is a great teacher because I learn something new from them. Everyone holds Great Wisdom that can Enlighten others, sometimes without knowing it. But, I personally don't Need to Follow anyone to learn something Grand from them. Nor do I wish anyone to follow me. Let us all walk side by side, SHARING and LEARNING from each other.

\* \* \*

(206)

When we talk about insanity, we use the expression 'out of our mind.' In reality, it is the confused thoughts and misinterpretations **within** the mind that are the seeds of insanity. We MEDITATE to stop our thinking or leave the mind. This is how we become CLEAR and FREE. This is how we become Enlightened. If only we were all 'Out of our Minds.'

\* \* \*

(207)

If just ONE person Cures themselves of a so-called 'incurable' dis-ease, so can you. If just ONE person Manifests Joy and Happiness, so can you. Yet, it may just take ONE person to put enough Doubt in your mind to believe you Can't. DO NOT buy into False Beliefs. It was YOUR Thoughts and Actions that Created the life you are living today. And YOU have the Power to Create the life You will live tomorrow, with your thoughts NOW.

\* \* \*

(208)

We are ALL of the same Source. This is why I say you can have a Great Relationship with ANYONE. Also, understand that you don't Need to find someone with whom you have Everything in common. Vive La Différence! Ultimately, for a Great Relationship you need only to find someone who has Love and Respect for THEMSELF. This is how they will likewise treat YOU.

\* \* \*

(209)

To Change the Life you're living, you must first Accept that YOU Created the Life you're living. It is indeed a Grand Responsibility. If this doesn't frighten or anger you, it may lead to the Wonderful Realization that YOU are the Creator. That YOU are the POWER you've been searching for. Love, Self-Empowerment, and Freedom to All.

\* \* \*

(210)

Once You find the courage to take Complete Responsibility for your life, there will be NO More Excuses, no one to blame. Every time you come up with an Excuse in Life, you Cheat yourself from a valuable Opportunity to Learn and Grow.

\* \* \*

(211)

Many see the NEW YEAR as the only opportunity to make big change in their lives. Yet, we know what often follows those New Year resolutions—procrastination! And, of course, this practice of procrastination has always set people up for failure. Rather, we must learn to see Each and Every day of the year as an Opportunity for Change. We must make Enlightenment an ongoing process, NOT a yearly resolution.

\* \* \*

(212)

While driving on the road of life, keep your focus on the road ahead, not the rear view mirror.

\* \* \*

(213)

Remember that the Spirit of a Holiday Season does **not** live in a shopping bag. It Lives in Your Heart and should be carried, not just for one week, but for Every Day of the year.

\* \* \*

(214)

All the Great Masters—Moses, Jesus, Buddha, Rama, Krishna, Muhammad, Chaitanya, Ramakrishna and more—taught the same basic Truths about LOVE. It is said that if you could put all the Great Masters in the same room, they would EMBRACE each other. However, if you put their Followers in the same room they may KILL each other.

DON'T BE A FOLLOWER.

BE a Unique Individual.

LIVE like a Master.

LOVE like a Master.

BE a Master.

\* \* \*

(215)

I believe in ME and you should believe in YOU. Don't be an extra; be a Star. Don't be a follower; be a Leader. Don't put anyone on a higher pedestal than yourself. To learn from another you must look into their eyes. Know your Power. Feel your Power. Believe your Power. No One is Greater than You.

\* \* \*

(216)

Trust in the journey, trust in the process of life. Believe that you are perfect. Believe that you are whole and complete. Believe that you are divinely guided. Know that you have chosen to be here. Know that your experiences here are simply lessons. Know that they are all for the highest good.

\* \* \*

(217)

We have created many restrictions in our lives. We have forced ourselves into little boxes with very limited views. We've created false ideas about Love to justify our dysfunctional behavior. We allow ourselves to be controlled by religious fear and politics. There really is only one way to find Peace and Freedom: Within our own Hearts.

Here in our hearts we are always Safe. Here, we don't need to follow anyone. Here, we are always Empowered. Here, we will be Enlightened. Here, we are always Loved. We must, of course, abide by the rules of society on the outside. But, on the inside we are Free to Think and Feel on the highest level.

Free Your mind. Free Your Heart. Free Your Spirit. Allow the Light to Shine in. This is how You will make the greatest change in the World

\* \* \*

(218)

Defeating another in a verbal or physical battle does **not** necessarily mean you have won. To ultimately evolve, your Spirit must come to terms with why it has Attracted this energy in the first place. Walk in Peace and Love.

\* \* \*

(219)

Controlling the Minds of others is relatively easy, especially those who live in weakened states of fear and anxiety. There are so many teachers, preachers, coaches, and similar who enjoy this FALSE sense of Power. TRUE POWER, however, is only achieved by Controlling our Own Minds and Empowering others to do the same.

\* \* \*

(220)

When you Truly learn to Love yourself, you may find yourself ALONE, but you will Never be LONELY. This is where you find your SOURCE. This is where you find your POWER. This is where you find your Peace. I under-

stand that this is a difficult concept to grasp at first, but
this is what you will come to KNOW.

\* \* \*

(221)

It's essential to Lighten Up now and again. It sets us
FREE. Even 'spiritual' people can get way too heavy.
I Celebrate my Spirituality, my Grand Connection to
Source, my Magic, and My Powers. But, I'm also here to
Experience being Human. So, here's to Sex and Choco-
late—not necessarily in that order.

\* \* \*

(222)

As soon as you label yourself you're stuck. You can't be
anything else. You stop growing. To evolve is to be constantly changing.

\* \* \*

(223)

It's actually quite Wonderful. Our blissful Spiritual Energy of Light can be felt through the physical sensation of a Sexual Orgasm. Well, unless your religion prohibits that desire ... Yes, of course I'm laughing. Only those fully asleep would deny themselves such an Incredible Pleasure that our Spirit manifested for enjoyment in the first place. It's like spending hours baking a delicious cake and then figuring out some reason that you're not allowed to taste it.

\* \* \*

(224)

You want Peace in the world, but have you found Peace within yourself? Each of the world's 10,000 religions and belief systems is sure the others are wrong. Ego and fear separate us from one another. We stubbornly hold onto these beliefs, as a fan stays loyal to a baseball team. But, when there are teams, one team always loses. This is not True Spirituality. This is a game, sometimes a deadly Game of War. There are those of us who choose not to have a team. And by doing this we create a FAMILY, a family that recognizes we all belong to each other; we are all from the Same Source. We are all one: This is **The New Way**.

\* \* \*

(225)

There's a big difference between Truth and Honesty. Each of us may have a different truth. Honesty, however, is about having the courage to express your Truth when asked for your opinion—not allowing Social, Religious, or Political Correctness to stifle you.

\* \* \*

(226)

TRUTH must be Discovered not learned. You are NOT what you've been Taught. So, who are you? First, you must step away from your self-image, your Roles, your Rules, and your Religions. You must Un-learn. Cleanse your mind. Here, you'll find Pure Consciousness. Here, you'll find Pure Spirit. Here, you'll find your True Nature. Here, you will find Yourself.

\* \* \*

(227)

The Universe is a Magnificent Bank. It not only gives back what you put in, but pays Huge Dividends.

\* \* \*

(228)

A true human who shows no Vulnerability is really the Most Vulnerable. They must always hide behind an inflated Ego. Arrogance becomes the Armor to shield any tenderness. The Truly Powerful Human Being has NO Fear of showing Vulnerability. This is Ultimate Confidence. This is the Real Strength that will Elevate themselves and others.

\* \* \*

(229)

You remain a Victim as long as you choose **not** to Learn from your Challenges. When you Choose to Learn and move forward, you become a Great Teacher to yourself and others.

\* \* \*

(230)

You don't need to better yourself. You just need to know yourself better.

\* \* \*

(231)

I only compete with myself. That way I always win.

\* \* \*

(232)

I'm often asked about my belief system or religion. I have NONE. The Universe is forever Evolving. I am forever Evolving. All belief systems and religions are set in their ways. For me life is about Expansion not Restriction. I prefer the Freedom of an Open, Detached mind—a mind that is forever changing. This is where you find Your TRUTH.

\* \* \*

(233)

Once you have experience True Self Esteem you will
never again concern yourself with being less or better
than another. Your Greatest Joy will come from BEING
who you are. Love and Respect yourself. You are simply
AMAZING.

# *Streams of Consciousness*

# *INDEX*

# In Closing

\* \* \*

I am most honored and grateful that you chose to read *The New Awakening*.

One never knows how another will receive or interpret their thoughts. My one hope is that you will understand true Self-Confidence and Self-Empowerment; that you will never have the need to follow anyone or anything, only the wisdom of your own heart.

Always *trust* in yourself. Always *believe* in yourself. Trust in the journey. Trust in the process of life. Trust that everything in life is just a lesson; that you are learning exactly as you need to.

I wish you a most powerful, positive journey. I wish you a life of fulfilled dreams. I wish you a happiness that comes from the deepest part of your soul to the farthest reaches of the Universe.

You are a Powerful, Bright and Beautiful Spirit. Know it. Feel it. Believe it.

Thank you with all my heart for allowing me to be a part of your journey.

With Love and Deepest Gratitude

*Eric Allen*

# *About the Author*

Eric Allen has devoted most of his 54 years to the Enlightenment and Self-Empowerment of men, women and children.

A Master Martial Artist with over 40 years experience, as well as a Fitness and Wellness expert, he was one of the top celebrity trainers in California for over 20 years.

His positive outlook on life is intoxicating. His powerful 'new age' philosophies, sense of humor, thoughts, and sayings have inspired people throughout the world to look at themselves and their beliefs in a very different light.

His message is clear: "Learn from everyone you meet, but follow no one." Eric says, "I'm not a Guru. I prefer people to walk beside me as equals, not sit at my feet."

In 2009 he wrote his first book **THE NEW WAY…The Ultimate Guide for Personal Power**, which has become one of the top sellers on Amazon Kindle.

You may also enjoy his website **<www.change-your-world.com>**, which is filled with beautiful, relaxing and empowering images, thoughts, and music.

18790924R00127

Made in the USA
San Bernardino, CA
29 January 2015